THE 5-MINUTE MEDITATOR

Quick meditations to calm your body and soothe your mind

ERIC HARRISON

First published in 2003 by
Judy Piatkus (Publishers) Limited
5 Windmill Street
London W1T 2JA
e-mail: info@piatkus.co.uk

A catalogue record for this book is available from the British Library

ISBN 0 7499 2459 4

Edited by Krystyna Mayer
Text design by the Bridgewater Book Company
Cartoons by Nik Scott

This book has been printed on paper manufactured with respect for the environment using wood from managed sustainable resources

Data manipulation by
Action Publishing Technology Ltd, Gloucester

Printed and bound in Great Britain by
Bookmarque Ltd, Croydon, Surrey

About the Author

Eric Harrison is one of Australia's most experienced meditation teachers. His approach is very practical and free from jargon. He has taught over 20,000 people at his meditation centre in Perth, Western Australia, and also works extensively in the corporate world. His books are now published in eight languages and ten countries and include the bestselling *Teach Yourself to Meditate* and *How Meditation Heals* (both Piatkus).

CONTENTS

Introduction xiii

PART ONE | THE BREATH AND THE BODY

1 To relax, get in touch with your body 2

2 The delicate art of sighing 8

3 The breath: your best ally against stress 12

4 Deep breathing 15

5 Breathing freely 20

6 Focusing, or paying attention 27

7 Sitting comfortably 33

8 Scanning the body 36

9 Coping with distractions 41

10 Walking meditations, part one 46

11 Meditating at the gym 55

12 Yoga and stretching 65

PART TWO | THE SENSES

13 To relax, be sensual 70

14 Food and drink 75

15 Just listening, nothing more than that 79

16 Look at the world around you 82

17 Where am I? Returning to the present 87

18 Where am I at? 89

19 Snapshot: the sensuality of little things 91

20 Walking meditations, part two 93

21 Affirmations: how words can help 97

PART THREE | ACTIVITIES

22 Pay attention to what you are doing 104

23 Household meditations 109

24 Going to the toilet 117

25 In the car 119

26 When you have to wait 125

27 How to fall asleep 130

PART FOUR | FINAL THOUGHTS

28 Am I doing it right? 138

29 What else can I do? 144

Exercises

Three Sighs 10

Deep Breathing while Sitting 18

Deep Breathing while Walking 19

Breathing Freely 26

Sitting Comfortably 34

Countdown 39

Body Scan 40

Naming the Distractions 44

Breathe through the Stretch 61

Relax into the Pose 61

Breathe between Poses 68

Food or Drink Meditation 78

Random Sounds 81

Visual Object Meditation 86

Where am I? 88

Where am I at? 90

Snapshot 92

Walking Meditations 96

Affirmations 101

Household Meditations 115

Going to the Toilet 117

Red Light Meditation 120

Driving meditation 124

Standing meditation 129

Two-minute nap 134

Falling asleep 135

Meditations

Three Sighs Revisited 49

Breathing Deeply 50

Walking Comfortably 51

Counting the Steps 53

Synchronised Breathing 54

Stop Before You Start 58

Coordinate Breathing and Strokes 58

The Perfect Stroke 59

Focus on the Active Muscles 60

Focus on Your Centre of Gravity 61

Stop at Exactly the Right Time 62

Pause Between Sets 63

Sounds 94

Visual Objects 94

Wind 95

Being Present 95

Introduction

MEDITATION IS WELL WORTH DOING. It relaxes the body and calms the mind rapidly; it is the best way to reduce stress; it improves your health and helps with many common illnesses; it makes your thinking clearer and more imaginative; it puts you in touch with your deeper emotions; it dispels sadness and confusion, and it makes sensory pleasures more enjoyable. It can bring peace, beauty and wisdom into your life.

So why don't we do it?

We don't seem to have the time. At the Perth Meditation Centre in Western Australia, I've taught meditation to some 20,000 people from all walks of life since 1987. I've taught business executives, housewives, tradesmen, little children and the elderly. I've trained doctors, psychologists and teachers to help others. I've taught top athletes and performers, and also the chronically ill and dying. I've taught in universities, on offshore oil rigs and in little country towns. My books are published in eight languages in ten countries. I estimate that half a million people worldwide have now read my books or used my instructional CDs.

My students usually tell me they enjoy the classes and understand the benefits, but I find that less than half of them continue with regular practice. The rest invariably say, 'I can't find the time' and, considering the lives they lead, they seem to have good excuses.

I've written *The 5-minute Meditator* specially for people who have no time to meditate – the ones who need it the most. Over the years, I've taught what I call 'spot meditations' that are very short and can be done anywhere and anytime. Many of them take no extra time at all, because they blend into other activities such as walking, eating or exercise. Others use the 'waste' time during the day, when you're waiting for something, or on public transport or trying to fall asleep at night. These practices are very popular, and many of my students say they are the only meditations they do.

These might seem like second-best meditations, but in fact several spot meditations a day are much more useful than one long one. Every meditation has an afterglow, where you remain fairly relaxed for the few minutes following it. So five short meditations give you five afterglows, whereas one long meditation has only one. The most productive meditations, minute for minute, are the short ones.

In fact, spot meditations have an ancient history. The Buddha himself said, 'meditate while walking, eating, dressing, lying down and going to the toilet'. These practices are designed to help you be calm and clear-minded not just when you meditate, but right through the day. They encourage you to 'be present' and simply pay attention to what you are doing, rather than thinking about a dozen things at once. If you do this, the benefits can be enormous.

Most books on managing stress won't help you when you're starved of time. They often suggest strategies that are more suitable for twenty-year-olds on their summer holidays. If you cannot find half an hour to sit quietly, how on earth would you fit in yoga exercises, long baths with aromatherapy oils (make sure you get the right ones!) and elegant visualisations? If you cannot cut down your hours at work or stop driving the kids around, where would you find those extra hours to attend a gym or get a massage regularly?

These spot meditations are different. Since they require no extra time, you don't have to squeeze them into your daily schedule. They also require no props – not even a quiet room, and certainly not soft music, incense or yoga mats. They can be done in any state of mind – the crazier and more stressed out the better. Nor do you have to stop what you are doing to practise them. You only have to learn how to do them. A well-paced, balanced life really is possible without enormous sacrifices.

HOW TO GET STARTED

Meditation is about choosing where you direct your attention. If you focus on something that is simple and sensual, you relax. If you focus on something stressful and complicated, such as your habitual thoughts, you remain tense. The basic instructions are: focus on the sensations of the present – sight, sound, smell, taste or touch – and let your thoughts pass by in the background.

Because the principles are so versatile, you can apply them in all kinds of circumstances. I'll offer you dozens of exercises in the following pages as starting points. Once you've tried a few, I suggest you creatively adjust them to suit your lifestyle and personality.

Part I of *The 5-minute Meditator* invites you to focus on the breath and the body. These practices give you an excellent foundation, since they help you recognise what tension and relaxation actually feel like in the body. Part II asks you to focus on sight, sound, smell, taste and touch, and enter the delicious world of eating and drinking meditations. Part III invites you to focus on more complex activities, such as cooking, housework, driving and so on.

To get the most from the book, I suggest you read it with big pauses. When you find a meditation that interests you, put down the book and do it. Try out as many exercises as you wish while you read. Once you find one you like, I suggest you do it repeatedly to get familiar with it.

You don't even need five minutes. Many of these exercises are only a minute or two long. They're all very simple and you can easily stretch them out in time as you wish. One or two minutes is all you need to destress rapidly and restore your equilibrium. Five minutes can relax you to the point of sleep, and ten minutes is pure luxury.

People who want to meditate often fail because they cannot find a suitable time ('too busy') or place ('too noisy'). In fact, you cannot expect a five-minute space to suddenly open before you. We automatically fill up any spaces with thought or activity, so you have to look out for them.

I suggest you repeatedly ask yourself the question: 'When could I meditate?' or even better, 'Can I meditate right now?' You could meditate while making breakfast; walking to your car or the train in the morning; standing in the supermarket queue; going to the toilet; eating lunch; doing exercise; sitting through a boring meeting; falling asleep at night. Frequency, by the way, is more important than length. Meditating for ten minutes three times a day is more productive than one thirty-minute meditation session.

Once you find a suitable meditation, it's almost essential to do it routinely for a few days at least – you need to do a meditation at least four times over four days for it to go into your long-term memory. This means that *every* time you walk to your car, or stand in a queue (for example), the thought arises: 'I can meditate now! I did it here yesterday and I can do it here again today.' This is how you develop your own repertoire of exercises.

You may find it hard to believe that these simple, opportunistic meditations can do much good. In fact, they can change you from a stressed, harassed and miserable individual into someone who copes beautifully and finds peace and pleasure in the most unexpected places.

Meditation is very simple, which is why it works. It simplifies our mental activity to an almost childlike degree. It's all about being in the present and focusing on the world of the senses. When you do something simple and sensual, the body automatically relaxes and the mind calms down. It's just a matter of making this happen much more deliberately than you usually would.

Personally, I do ten or twenty spot meditations a day, and I think I would have gone mad without them. They destress me rapidly and bring beauty and intelligence into my ordinary working day. I do spot meditations to revitalise my soul, just as I do physical exercise to keep my body healthy.

I would love to see you pick up this skill and make it your own. Once you get the knack, spot meditations are amazingly versatile and easy to do. I've seen them transform the lives of so many people who never do longer, more formal, meditations. You simply have to understand how they work, and creatively shape them to your purposes. These modest and self-effacing practices can eventually give you results that are little short of miraculous. I see it happen for my students all the time, and I know it can happen for you. I wish you all the best with the meditations.

Eric Harrison
April 2003
www.perthmeditationcentre.com.au

PART ONE

THE BREATH AND THE BODY

1. To relax, get in touch with your body

MEDITATION CAN SEEM very complicated. People meditate for a variety of reasons: to relax, to heal cancer, to get rich, to find their inner self, to play sport better, to speak to God or to fall asleep! Meditation also comes in many flavours – Hindu, Buddhist, Christian and New Age – and frequently promises the earth.

Yet most meditation practices are very similar beneath the surface. You could say they are a thousand different expressions of the same underlying principles. They all at least start by relaxing the body and calming the mind (though some do this better than others).

In fact, body and mind are so closely connected that you can actually regard them as one organism. If your body relaxes, your mind calms down. Similarly, if your mind calms down, your body relaxes. It is almost impossible to imagine the opposite: being physically relaxed while your mind is agitated, for example.

Since physical relaxation is so pivotal to meditation, it helps to understand exactly what it is. Tension and relaxation, in fact, are the sympathetic and parasympathetic responses of the central nervous system. Tension is the 'fight-or-flight' response that turns *on* adrenalin and cortisol, giving us maximum energy to face a crisis. Relaxation is the reverse process that turns *off* the stress hormones, letting us return to balance. Meditation therefore turns *off* the 'stress response' and turns *on* the 'relaxation response'.

These two responses naturally alternate during the day according to how much energy we need. It's like using the accelerator pedal in a car to go faster or slower. You press it down when you're busy, and you ease up, or use the brakes, when you want to go slower. The stress response makes you go faster, and the relaxation response slows you down. At any time during the day, you're either speeding up and burning energy, or slowing down and conserving it.

When you're very anxious, the pedal is flat to the floor. That's when you burn a lot of energy, go nowhere very fast and often crash. Do you know that feeling? I certainly do. That's why I originally learnt to meditate, thirty-three years ago.

TWO KINDS OF RELAXATION

People usually think of 'deep relaxation' as a state that is almost unconscious. In fact, when you meditate, you often hover in a beautiful place where you are not quite asleep or awake: you are balancing on the threshold between the two. In this state, all the biological systems in your body return to balance. Tight muscles soften, the racing heart slows down, the digestive system starts working again, and so on.

Yet we also talk about relaxation in another way. If you say, 'I had a relaxing day,' this doesn't mean you were drowsy all day long. It means you were cruising along, pacing yourself well and enjoying yourself. This is a balanced state where you're not burning unnecessary energy or pushing your body to its limits.

It happens naturally when you are 'in the present'. This is when you are just 'doing what you are doing' and not thinking about a dozen other things as well – in other words, when you are paying attention to one thing at a time, you usually feel relaxed as well.

The spot meditations are designed to help you return to this state of equilibrium whenever you need to. When you are in balance throughout the whole day, you are at ease with yourself and the world. It's the complete opposite of a 'stressful' or 'difficult' day, when one crisis seems to succeed another and your body pays the price.

RELAXING A LITTLE IS A GOOD THING TO DO

We can also think of the tension–relaxation cycle as having several settings, like the volume control on a stereo. From maximum to minimum these go something like this: 'Panic. Stress. Balance. Relaxation. Sleep'.

You don't have to relax deeply for a meditation to be worthwhile. If you suffer a panic attack, it's a great relief to go from 'Panic' to 'Stress'. Similarly, if you're stressed, it can feel quite wonderful to come down a notch into 'Balance'.

You can shift from 'Panic' to 'Stress', or from 'Stress' to 'Balance', very quickly if you know how. Since stress is painful, the body has a strong instinct to escape it. All it needs is a little encouragement, and just a few seconds of a spot meditation can do it. For example, if you stop what you are doing, take stock, take a few deep breaths and sigh, you can relax markedly in less than a minute. I have included an exercise that explains how to do this on page 10.

TUNE INTO YOUR BODY

Because relaxation is such a physical event, it's very useful to be consciously aware of your body. This seems obvious, and yet many meditation practices, such as visualisation or mantra for example, virtually ignore the body or take it for granted. Such practices can be somewhat weak as a consequence.

In fact, the people who suffer most from anxiety are those who are out of touch with their bodies. They often feel they're coping perfectly well, since they manage to do everything they have to do, but they cannot understand why they also have panic attacks, insomnia, hypertension or digestive problems.

If you make friends with your body and listen to what it tells you, the advantages are huge. To put it in a nutshell, awareness heals. If you become aware of tensions in your face and shoulders, for example, it's easy to soften them within seconds. If you're not conscious of them, they stay tight, often for a lifetime (I'm not exaggerating). The same applies to the other strains and imbalances in your body.

If you're aware of your body, you'll know exactly where you are on that sliding scale between tension and relaxation, and how to shift from one to the other. You'll also know whether a meditation is working or not, because you will be able to read the signs of success in your body.

READING THE SIGNS OF RELAXATION

Some people tell me 'I haven't felt relaxed for years.' It's an alien experience for them. It is a sad truth that even in sleep their muscles are tight and they're grinding their teeth. They

... to face yet another miserable day

wake up exhausted to face yet another miserable day. It's not surprising that stress, fatigue and depression go hand in hand.

Even if you're less stressed than this, you may only have a vague idea of what it feels like to be relaxed. When we do relax, our minds tend to wander and space out, so we're not conscious enough to notice how we feel. We're not there to enjoy it! Or you may be a person whose nervous system only has an on-off switch, with no sliding scale in between. When you're awake, you're tense. When you relax at all, you fall asleep.

If you want to relax, it's very helpful to know the territory you're trying to enter. Meditation is often described as a 'relaxed and alert' state, and this very alertness helps you to relax more fully. If you can recognise the biological markers of relaxation, you can use them as leverage to take you deeper.

When you sit still to relax, it seems as if you're doing nothing. In fact, massive changes are occurring inside you and some are quite obvious.

Relaxation Response

1. Your muscles start to soften. The adrenalin charge fades, and all the muscles throughout your body start to sag. This is most obvious in your face and shoulders. Overall, your body starts to feel heavy or still. If you focus on this heavy feeling, you accelerate the effect.
2. Your circulation improves and there is an increased blood flow to the skin, which often feels slightly tingly and warm. Your skin feels more alive, the way it does after a shower or aerobic exercise or a shot of alcohol. Your digestion can start ticking over as well.
3. The adrenalin and endorphins you produce when tense – natural opiates that tend to numb our bodies – fade away when you relax, and you often start to feel the little aches and pains and fatigue they were masking. When you feel

the headache or sore neck, these are good signs that you are relaxing, so don't fight them. Just let them surface and do what they want to do.

4. Your breathing changes dramatically when you relax. When tense, we usually over-breathe from the upper chest. As we relax, we let the breath go, so it feels deep. And when we relax fully, the breath usually becomes light and delicate. I'll explain this in more detail in the coming chapters.

Because it's so useful to know what tension and relaxation actually feel like, this book starts with breath and body meditations. These give you an excellent foundation and blend very well with the more varied meditations that follow. As I explain in later chapters, you really can relax by focusing on a leaf or sandwich, or while ironing clothes. However, when you do so, it helps if you can use your body as a yardstick. If you occasionally check how your body feels, you'll know whether you are actually relaxing or not.

2. THE DELICATE ART OF SIGHING

ONE OF MY STUDENTS was trying to persuade a high-flying executive friend to relax. 'Just stop and take seven deep breaths,' he said. 'Don't be silly. I haven't got the time!' she wailed.

If you have time to breathe, you have time to do the next meditation. It is called 'Three Sighs' and it takes only thirty seconds to a minute to do. I do it several times a day and it works like magic. It's a natural circuit-breaker. It gets me out of my head and brings me back to earth immediately.

Sighing is the perfect physiological antidote to stress because it reverses the way we breathe when we're anxious. Tension, which is the fight-or-flight response, wires us up to react rapidly to a perceived danger. By breathing tightly, or by holding our breath, we can stay charged up. We definitely don't sigh in a dangerous situation, because that releases the tension and makes us vulnerable to attack. At the end of a sigh, the body and mind are too loose to respond quickly to anything.

Sighs happen naturally when you're relaxing, or about to relax. Like yawns, they signal a shift towards relaxation or even sleep. Sighs and yawns are involuntary, but they occur only when something in the mind lets go. At that moment, you unconsciously realise the crisis is over and you can relax.

Both the body and the mind become more loose and open as you sigh. By *consciously* sighing, as you do in this exercise, you send a signal from your body back to your mind, saying 'It's okay to relax now. See? I'm sighing.' A sigh is the fastest way to initiate the relaxation response, so let's analyse why it's so effective.

THE THREE STAGES OF A SIGH

You'll notice that a sigh has these three stages: the in-breath, the out-breath and the pause at the end. If you practise, you can become much better at each of them.

1. When you are tense, the upper chest and neck muscles are bound to be tight. That's virtually the signature sensation of anxiety. However the first part of a sigh – the deep in-breath – stretches and opens up those muscles. It's much easier for muscles to loosen if you can stretch them out first. Furthermore, tense breathing is usually fast and shallow, and the deep, slow tempo of a sigh is the complete opposite of that. A sigh breaks the rhythm of tight breathing.
2. The actual sigh itself – the out-breath – is long and loose and gentle. It doesn't stop until it's complete and all the air has left the lungs. It has a feeling of lazy abandonment about it.
3. A genuine sigh doesn't hurry through to the next in-breath. It has a pause at the end, where everything stops for a few seconds. If there wasn't a pause, it wouldn't be a sigh at all. It would just be a deep breath. Brief as it is, this pause can be a place of complete stillness, where you really find the meaning of the word 'tranquillity'. It's a lovely place to rest and temporarily escape the merry-go-round of your thoughts.

In fact, a perfectly executed sigh is a work of art. The in-breath is full and expansive. The out-breath is luxurious and total, and the pause at the end seems to last forever. The perfect sigh is just as elegant and satisfying, in its own small way, as a beautiful tennis stroke.

Simple as it is, you can still sigh badly! When you breathe in, make sure you activate the belly and the diaphragm as much as the upper body. When you breathe out, let the breath drop as far as it wants to go, but don't force it. Even though the pause feels lovely, don't try to protract it. Be relaxed! Let the new in-breath come when it wants to.

After three or four breaths, you'll probably feel your whole body relaxing in sympathy with the breath. Yet because sighing is an unnatural way to breathe, three sighs is usually enough, and it's then best to let your breathing resume a natural rhythm again. Or you can move into the Deep Breathing exercise described in Chapter 4.

Three Sighs is a classical spot meditation in that it can be done anywhere, anytime, in any position or activity, and with the eyes open or closed. It's so versatile and portable that everyone should do regularly.

I commonly do it whenever I stand up and start to walk somewhere. I particularly use it when I get out of my car or go out of my front door. After I've been sitting for a while, my body is usually somewhat slumped and my breathing is restricted. So when I start to walk, I sigh three times to reconstruct my posture and free up my breathing. In those moments, I also blow away my thoughts and get my mind clear for the next activity.

Three Sighs

Breathe in deeply*, opening the belly and lower ribs.*

Breathe out completely. Let it all go.

Rest in the pause, feeling the belly soften a little more.
Hold the pause until you really have to breathe again.

Repeat two more times.

Notice that each breath is usually deeper than the last. Three or four sighs are usually enough.

Now let your breathing resume its natural rhythm, noticing how different it feels.

3. THE BREATH: YOUR BEST ALLY AGAINST STRESS

PARADOXICALLY, THE BEST WAY to relax is to notice exactly how tense you feel. If you realise that your shoulders are up around your ears, or that you are holding your breath, you don't have to think what to do next. Your shoulders automatically drop and you start breathing again. The awareness alone has a magical effect, reminding you that it's your choice whether to hold on or to let go.

If you get into the habit of checking whether you are tense or relaxed 'right now', you will soon be able to recognise how tense you feel. The signs of tension may be quite obvious: a rigid body, anxious mind, aching shoulders and knotted stomach. However, the clearest indicator of all is the breath. It gives you an instant printout.

If you notice your breathing is tense, you only need a few sighs or deep breaths to start relaxing it. Your facial muscles and belly are likely to soften at the same time. As your breathing loosens up, it has a ripple effect, acting as a guide and example for the rest of the body to follow.

The breathing mechanism is easy to relax because, unlike most of our musculature, it is within our conscious control. We only need to sigh, or breathe deeply a few times, to trigger the relaxation response within seconds. If you've done the Three Sighs exercise (*see page 10*), you'll know how effective this is. Of course, you cannot sigh forever, so the next two chapters give you ways of meditating on the breath for longer periods.

The breath is such a fundamental tool that you'll find dozens of different breathing exercises in the Yogic and Buddhist traditions. If you simply want to relax, it's not imperative to do the formal exercises. However, the more you understand the breath, the more useful it becomes. Since it's almost impossible to relax deeply without some awareness of breathing, let's look at it in more detail before doing the exercises and meditations in the following chapters.

Breathing is quite a complex action. It's much more than a simple in–out. When things go wrong, the breath gets jerky or constricted, or becomes too shallow or too fast. In fact, there are many gradations between the frantic breathing of panic, and the oceanic rhythms of deep sleep. Let me explain how the tension–relaxation cycle is mirrored in the breath, so you can see how one stage moves on to the next.

TENSE BREATHING

When you're shocked or startled, you naturally **freeze** and hold your breath. It's what a gazelle does when it senses a predator nearby.

The next stage, the **arousal**, involves rapid, shallow, upper-body breathing, which is typical of people who suffer panic attacks. This hyperventilation causes more in-breathing than out-breathing, and floods the body with the oxygen it needs to metabolise energy quickly.

If the gazelle now **flees**, its breathing becomes very deep and regular, using the energy raised in the arousal stage. Similarly, we're likely to go into bursts of deep breathing when faced with demanding situations for several minutes. This steady, deep breathing gives us the energy we need to get through such events.

Each stage – the freeze, the arousal and the flight – is appropriate at the right time. Unfortunately, we can get stuck in any one of them. Even though the last stage, the deep regular breathing, is obviously better than the first two, we can still overdo it. If you over-oxygenate yourself, you'll burn more energy than you need and soon get exhausted.

RELAXED BREATHING

Tense breathing is governed by the stress response of the nervous system. But as the relaxation response kicks in, the breathing goes into reverse. The next three stages are: sighing, relaxed breathing and no-breath.

The first of these is the sigh (*see page 9*). We let go of tension by involuntarily sighing, and the out-breaths becomes longer than the in-breaths. This is the exact opposite of the hyperventilation (short out-breaths) that occurs in the arousal stage.

The sighing gradually subsides into natural, relaxed breathing. I'll encourage you to get very familiar with this, so you'll know whether you're truly relaxed or not. Relaxed breathing usually feels *rhythmic* but not *regular,* just as each wave breaking on a shore is a little different from the one before and after. It is usually gentle and delicate, with the odd sigh and little 'catch-up' breaths thrown in. I'll describe this more fully in Chapter 5.

Finally, when you're very relaxed, the breath can literally stop for many seconds at a time. It becomes very quiet and subtle, and there can be long pauses between the out-breath and the in-breath. It's a delightful, serene feeling when *everything* goes still. This no-breath most commonly occurs when you are so relaxed that you are almost asleep. It is the exact opposite of the frozen breath of panic that occurs at the *top* of the in-breath.

Chapter 4 explains how to breathe deeply in order to relax. Because you take in a lot of air as you do this, it is best done while you are walking or doing some activity. Chapter 5 talks about the natural, relaxed kind of breathing that occurs in a longer sitting meditation.

4. Deep breathing

LET ME SCARE YOU A LITTLE. Do you often have tight neck, shoulder and chest muscles, and suffer from headaches and insomnia? These are the classical signs of anxiety disorders, chronic fatigue syndrome (Myalgic Encephalomyelitis or ME) and, to a lesser degree, depression. You may not be quite that bad yet, but those symptoms only get worse unless you do something about it. They won't vanish on their own. I see the long-term consequences in my classes every week.

Well over 90 per cent of people who suffer from these disorders will also breathe poorly. Their breaths are typically fast, shallow and jerky, and only involve the upper chest. Their chest, neck and shoulder muscles become tight and painful, and never relax significantly, even in sleep. A chronically anxious person won't even be able to breathe deeply. Years of stress can make their body into a prison, so that their lungs will be quite unable to expand to their full capacity.

Chronic stress and poor breathing are virtually identical. It doesn't matter whether one causes the other or vice versa, because they are inseparable in their effect on the body. Fortunately the cure is also obvious, though rarely developed systematically except in the yoga tradition. If you want to start relieving stress, open up your torso and breathe more freely. It's as simple as that. If you do this systematically and mindfully, the results can be better than any anti-depressants or painkillers.

Of course, we cannot focus on our breathing all day long, but then we don't need to. Just a few minutes of deep breathing each day can make a huge difference to our well-being. Our lung capacity steadily shrinks as we get older and breathe less.

In fact, elderly people barely breathe at all and their lungs become full of fluid, which is why they often die of minor respiratory illnesses. We can help to keep ourselves young by expanding our lungs to their full capacity at least once a day – it holds the ageing process at bay.

When you fill the body with air, you stretch the chest muscles the same way the surface of a balloon is stretched when you blow it up. Over time, this gradually expands those muscles beyond their former limits and makes them more supple. Done systematically, this can reverse the effects of years of tension, opening the chest and virtually rebuilding the structure of your body.

Breathing literally massages the body from the inside. The up and down motion of the diaphragm gently lifts and lowers the organs in the belly, helping to aerate them and keep them healthy. Both organs and muscles need to be supple to take in oxygen and to let the waste products out. A well-aerated body is much healthier and feels less pain, and usually feels more cheerful as well.

Generally, if one part of the body relaxes the rest of it does too. You're likely to find other muscles loosening in sympathy with the breath, even when they're not directly involved. Deep breathing, sighing and yawning are very similar in effect, and all trigger a ripple effect of muscle relaxation throughout the body.

It's all so simple! What makes it a meditation is that you pay attention to what you are doing and try to do it well. In other words, you don't just huff and puff a bit while thinking of other things. It's quite possible to work out aerobically and still breathe tightly while doing so. A single breath actually involves an array of different muscles throughout your torso, all working in coordination. It takes some attention and effort to breath harmoniously, but the more you do so, the more satisfying it becomes.

DEEP, SMOOTH AND NATURAL BREATHING

So can you breathe deeply, smoothly and naturally? For our purposes, a deep breath involves fully expanding the diaphragm and the lower ribs, but *not* the upper chest. To relax, you need to minimise the upper body breathing that is so typical of anxious people, at least until the lower body comes to life. People who suffer from anxiety attacks are often trained to breathe through the lower body to reverse the effect – in other words to practise anti-anxiety breathing.

Relaxing Rapidly

1. Keep your attention low in the body. Push out the belly and the lower ribs as you breathe in. It can help to think of the breathing action as going out and in on the horizontal plane, rather than vertically up and down. If your shoulders rise and fall significantly as you breathe deeply, or if your chest moves before your belly does, you'll simply reinforce the habit of anxious breathing, even if you're taking in a lot of air. You'll also be unable to sigh or breathe out fully because the belly will remain tight.
2. Try to make the breath smooth, in the sense that it flows easily like the motion of a wave. Breathing is usually an automatic process, but if you focus on it, you'll find you can make the coordination smoother and more luxurious.
3. Keep the breathing as natural as possible. Don't try to force the breath or make it perfectly regular. Coax it to be slow and low in the body, but don't manhandle it. Let each breath take the shape and time that feels natural to it. Rest a little at the end of the out-breath, and wait for the new in-breath to come when it wants to.

You'll find that natural breathing is typically a bit erratic, yet it feels quite pleasant anyway.

If you breathe deeply in a sitting position, about two or three minutes is usually enough. Deep breathing can over-oxygenate the body and give you more energy than you need for the task of just sitting still. This can make you feel a bit jumpy and wanting to move, rather than relaxed. So after two or three minutes, let the deep breathing go and don't control your breath at all – this is what I call 'breathing freely'. I describe this more fully in the next chapter (*see page 26*).

Deep Breathing while Sitting

Sigh *three or four times to open up your breathing: big in-breath, full out-breath and the pause at the end.*

Breathe deeply *and slowly for two or three minutes.*

Focus on moving out the lower ribs and the belly.

Make sure the shoulders are not rising and falling.

Think horizontally: 'out, in', not 'up, down'.

Let go completely on each out-breath.
Pause as long as you like at the end.

Eventually let the breath be 'free': don't control it at all.

Stay quiet by gently watching the breath as long as you like.

Deep Breathing, however, works perfectly as a meditation while you are walking, since you're actually using the extra energy that the breathing provides. As you'll see later, there are many ways to relax while you walk, but Deep Breathing is a good way to start. I suggest you aim for at least five minutes of Deep Breathing a day, while you walk. The health benefits alone, through fully aerating the lungs on a regular basis, can be enormous.

Deep Breathing while Walking

Choose your place: a quiet street or a park is best.

Walk deliberately at your usual pace.

Make your breathing deep, smooth and rhythmic.

Notice your surroundings, but keep your focus inside.

Feel how your body becomes more rhythmic as you walk.

Notice how your breathing tightens up whenever you slip back into thought.

5. Breathing freely

MEDITATORS EVENTUALLY DISCOVER this wonderful truth: you don't have to make yourself relax. You just stand back and let it happen. Meditation is the art of doing nothing. It is a kind of deliberate 'non-doing' and 'non-thinking'. Your body and mind will naturally settle if you give them half a chance. The less you try to do, the better it works!

Of course, it's rare for us to be so inactive. Our minds want to stay busy even if our bodies are still. It goes against our nature, and our Western culture, to simply 'be' rather than 'do'. Even if you're sitting still, your mind could still be running around in circles. It takes a little effort and discipline to resist our habit of mental busyness.

Of course, letting go and doing nothing is easier said than done. Even our bodies like to stay busy. If you are anxious, your muscles are working hard to stay tense, burning lots of energy and wearing you out. They are like sentry guards that can fall asleep while standing up, still holding their rifles.

Those muscles in the face, shoulders, stomach and hands can hold on indefinitely unless you visit them one by one and say, 'The war is over. Put aside your rifle now and lie down.' Often, they say, 'Don't worry about me! I feel just fine as I am!' It can take some time for them to let go of their vigilance.

We usually feel we have to 'do' something to relax, but in fact the opposite is true. We simply notice when the body and mind are toiling away unnecessarily and invite them to stop. This kind of skilful 'non-doing' also applies to meditating on the breath. The Three Sighs and the Deep Breathing exercises I have just described are both a kind of doing, albeit of a gentle kind. They break the tension and start you relaxing but, at a certain point, it feels right to stop controlling the breath altogether.

STOP CONTROLLING THE BREATH

When you simply watch what the breath does, without trying to shape it, you are doing what I call 'free breathing', or 'breathing freely'. By this means you don't try to make the breaths long or deep or regular. You simply give each breath space to do whatever it wants to do.

The breath in fact has many moods. It can be jerky or smooth, shallow or deep, constricted or fluid. You could breath from the chest or the diaphragm or the belly. Many of these kinds of breathing are signs of stress, and the controlled breathing exercises I have given you are designed to even them out. Because tension locks up the body, we can't go immediately into free breathing: it's too subtle. We need a few sighs or deep breaths to kick-start the process first.

Even when you are relaxed, the breath continues to change, though in more subtle ways. There are many stages between the frozen breath of shock and the abandoned breathing of deep sleep, so don't expect to relax instantly. Even a single thought of pleasure or sadness can change the breathing immediately. In fact, every breath is unique, and mirrors exactly your state of mind in the moment.

The body has a profound instinct for what is healthy and comfortable. It knows exactly how it wants to breathe, and it will unerringly move towards free, open, spontaneous breathing if you give it half a chance. Your discipline is to interfere as little as possible and let the process unfold. Usually, you cannot help controlling the breath to some degree whenever you focus on it, but ideally you control it as little as possible. It is quite okay, though, to gently shape the breaths to make them more smooth and satisfying.

Basically, you follow the pleasure principle. Free breathing has a sensual, luxurious quality about it. You let *everything* go as you breathe out – the breath, muscle tension, thoughts and worries – and enjoy the sublime laziness of this. You are gradually moving towards the effortless breathing of a sleeping child.

Of course, you can still encourage the process a little. As you relax, you'll detect small, residual tensions you never noticed at first – places where the muscles are still holding on. When the big tensions go, the smaller ones automatically come to the surface. You can use the rhythmic motion of the breath to gently massage those points of constriction and open them up.

You can also maximise the feeling of release as you breathe out. Rest in the pause at the end, and don't hurry the in-breath. Let each breath have its little peculiarities. Don't try to make the breaths even, or to eliminate the 'catch-up' breaths.

IN SEARCH OF TRANQUILLITY

Eventually this free breathing leads you into states of deep tranquillity. It seems a shame to analyse what tranquility actually is, but unless we do, it's likely to remain somewhat vague and unattainable. We need to translate it from a beautiful concept into a physical reality.

Among other things, tranquillity is a feeling in the body. If the body is not calm and still, the mind is unlikely to be either. You feel most tranquil when you're deeply relaxed but still alert. You relax more fully if you fall asleep, but in that state you're not conscious enough to appreciate it, and your mind could still be turbulent under the surface.

At the edge of sleep, the body slows down and becomes very still. Of course, 'stillness' is a relative term, since the body never really stops. Respiration, digestion, the heart and all the other systems keep ticking over, but with a difference: they burn considerably less energy than when the body is tense. As we relax, every muscle and body function seeks out its natural state of equilibrium, and we move into the natural rhythms of our own bodies.

But relaxation alone doesn't make us tranquil. Everyone relaxes, since that is the biological process that takes us to sleep, but not everyone becomes tranquil. Many of us are so stressed and exhausted that when we start to relax, we collapse into a restless sleep.

You find tranquillity only if you can pause on that threshold between wakefulness and sleep. A tranquil mind is still and clear. As is the case with the body, this stillness is relative, since consciousness is always mobile, but a tranquil mind is infinitely more settled than a mind that is in its usual waking or sleeping state.

... it also feels delightful

A tranquil mind still moves but very slowly. You can place it where you want and it stays there. It feels spacious and detached. It is lucid and passively observant. It doesn't want to go anywhere or do anything. It feels at one with the body and is not in conflict with anything. It also feels delightful. A tranquil mind mirrors the soft, sensual feeling of the relaxed body.

TRANQUILLITY AT THE END OF THE BREATH

The body and mind are most still at the end of the out-breath. When you do the Three Sighs exercise, you'll find there's a space between the end of the sigh and the next in-breath. In that space, everything stops for a few seconds where the relaxation is total. When you have a really satisfying sigh, all the muscles soften and the mind lets go completely. You get your first taste of real tranquillity in that space between the breaths.

Once you recognise that space, you'll find you can stay there longer if you keep your mind settled. Have you ever tried to hold your breath for a long time underwater? The secret is to become very still, mentally and physically. I used to lie on the bottom of a swimming pool almost in a trance, not thinking or doing anything, just waiting for the moment when I'd have to burst to the surface again.

If your mind is restless, your body will be too and there won't be a pause at the end of the breath. Yet you cannot force the breath to stop because that creates strain – quite the opposite of the relaxed, open feeling you want. So resting in that space between the breaths has to be done quite gently. It is like holding something soft and delicate, such as a butterfly, in your hands. You are inviting, but not forcing, the breath to stop and the mind to settle there.

As you relax more fully, you'll find that the space between the breaths gradually expands in time or, alternatively, that the breathing as a whole feels almost as calm as the space itself.

When you're calm, you actually breathe very little, since your body needs hardly any energy when you're at rest. The breaths can be almost imperceptible. In this state, they typically become very light and delicate, and often stop for long periods. The breathing ebbs and flows like the lapping of small waves on the shore of a lake.

As you move from high tension to deep rest, each stage on the way is mirrored by the breath. The tight, upper body breathing of anxiety gives way to sighs and deeper breathing. The breath gradually becomes free and loose, and you sink into even deeper states of tranquillity. Subtle as this is, you'll know when you're there. That state of physical and mental calm is unmistakeable and delightful.

STRUCTURING A BREATH MEDITATION

Because the relaxed breath can be quite subtle and evasive, it is good to use a verbal prop to keep you focused. You could say the words 'in ... out ...' as you breathe, and say a one- or two-word affirmation repeatedly (see Chapter 21 for more details).

Alternatively, you could count the breaths: count up to four, or eight, or ten breaths repeatedly, saying each number on each out-breath: '1 ... 2 ... 3 ... etc.' If you lose the count, it's a clear sign that you're drifting back into thought. Counting breaths is a very common way to anchor your mind in a meditation.

It should be possible to relax to the point of sleep in about five minutes, if you're at all tired. At first, you'll need to encourage the body to relax with a few sighs and deep breathing. At the end, however, you'll need almost no control at all: the breath can be free.

We've now looked at three breathing exercises: Three Sighs, Deep Breathing and Breathing Freely. The first takes less than a minute. The second takes two or three minutes, and the third can be as long as you like.

These three exercises also combine very well. Three Sighs is good for a very short meditation. For a two- or three-minute meditation, you do Three Sighs, followed by Deep Breathing. For a longer session, you can add one more exercise to the sequence, so that you get Three Sighs + Deep Breathing + Breathing Freely.

Breathing Freely

Sigh *three or four times to open up the body.*

Now ***breathe deeply*** *for a minute or two.*

When you feel ready, let the breath be free.

Don't try to control the breaths. Let each breath take its own shape, and try to feel the exact end and start of each breath.

Count the breaths to four, or eight or ten, repeatedly, or say the words, 'in, out', as you breathe.

Enjoy the sensual movement of the breath: feel it massage the body from inside.

Go to the points of constriction and 'breathe through' them.

Notice detail. Feel time slow down.

Enjoy the feeling of your body relaxing.

6. Focusing, or paying attention

WE CANNOT BUY TRANQUILLITY, even though there's an abundance of products available that promises just that. There *is* a cure for stress, but unfortunately it's a skill rather than a product we can purchase or a pill we can swallow. We all have this skill to some degree, and take it for granted, but we rarely cultivate it deliberately.

It's the art of focusing, or paying attention. If you focus on something simple or pleasant, your mind slows down and you automatically relax. Alternatively, if your mind is not focused, and you think at random about everything under the sun, you'll often feel stressed and confused, and may never relax at all.

We tend to blame our stress on external factors such as a busy life, physical pain or noise, but the ultimate cause is much simpler: our minds are too busy. We think too much. Much as we love and need to think, we overdo it. That endless stream of worries, fantasies, plans and inner dialogues stimulates our bodies and minds. We become think-aholics, at the mercy of our mental dramas.

So how does thinking give you high blood pressure or keep you awake at night? The emotions *behind* the thoughts are to blame. Some variant of fear, anger or desire drives most of our thoughts. For example, fear may be driving your thoughts about work. Anger may underpin your thoughts about your family. Desire may drive your planning for the weekend or the future.

These emotions mildly stimulate the stress response all day long. They chug along under the surface, sending a steady drip-feed of hormonal signals to the body, saying, 'This is no time to relax! We've got things to sort out first.' Our ordinary level of thinking pumps out quite enough adrenalin to keep us habitually tense, day after day and year after year. Every thought fuels the fire a little more. Therefore to relax at all, we need to distance ourselves from the habit of thinking.

ESCAPE INTO THE PRESENT

But how can we stop thinking? How can we stop our habitual tendency to think about a dozen things at once? It's virtually impossible to blank out thoughts or finish them off. If you've ever tried those options, you'll know how futile they are. However, just as antelopes can live safely in the company of lions, so we can keep a distance between ourselves and our thoughts, if we know how.

The strategy is simple: we focus on something else. Since most of our thoughts involve the past and future, we can escape them by focusing on the present moment. This basically means tuning into the world of the senses. We shift the mind from thinking mode to sensing mode.

'Sensing' means paying close attention to sight, sound, smell, taste or touch. This is the secret formula behind most meditations: come into the present by focusing on something sensual. Feel the breath, taste the coffee, enjoy the evening clouds, sense your own body as you sit or walk. Become a connoisseur of the here and now.

Most of us know this instinctively. We often choose to relax by doing sensual things. When stressed, we have a cup of tea or something to eat. To relax, we may listen to music, do exercise, walk in the park or play with a cat. In that moment when we truly taste the cake we're not thinking about yesterday or tomorrow. This disarms our usual thoughts and lets us relax. Meditation is simply a way of doing this more consciously.

FOCUSING ON ONE THING TO STAY PRESENT

Nearly all meditations have similar instructions. To stay in the present, they get you to focus on *one thing* in the present. We call this the meditation object. It's your anchor. It's what you persuade your mind to return to when it wanders away.

Meditations have different names, which are dependent on what the chosen focus is. If you focus on the breath, it's called a breath meditation. If you scan the body, it's a body-scanning meditation. If you listen to sounds, it's a sound meditation. If you look at a candle, it's a fire meditation. If you say a word or phrase repeatedly, it's an affirmation or a mantra meditation. The underlying instructions are the same for all of them: 'Focus on the meditation object and let everything else go'.

This is easier said than done. The 'everything else' includes all the other thoughts, sensations, memories, images and feelings that stream through the mind. Ideally, you notice them stream by without engaging them. Some thoughts, however, stick to you like glue. Some sweep you away like a stampeding herd. Some are gently seductive and whisper in your ear, and some just want to talk and talk and talk ...

We can call this 'the mind stream' or 'the stream of consciousness'. It never stops, even in deep sleep. Meditation doesn't dry up the stream. It just diverts most of your attention away from it, to keep it in the background. You cannot stop noticing thoughts, but it's your choice whether to drop the meditation object and engage them or not.

Meditation in fact involves two skills: focusing and awareness. **Focusing** is relatively easy to understand. It's the art of putting one thought, sensation or activity in the foreground, and returning to it when you get distracted.

Awareness is a more subtle skill. Since you cannot block out thoughts, you learn instead to notice them passively, without responding to them. You notice thoughts come and go in the background, while you predominantly focus on something sensual in the foreground. This is the art of 'watching with detachment' or 'being an observer'. It works much better than trying to ignore thoughts completely.

A TYPICAL MEDITATION

So what usually happens when you meditate? Let's assume you decide to focus on the breath, breathing deeply for the two or three minutes it takes you to walk to the shops. You tune into the breath, and feel it rise and fall. You feel the body expanding and contracting. You're in the present and in the world of the senses, so you naturally start to relax.

However, the mind is full of temptations. After a few seconds, it says 'Okay, I've got that. What else shall I do while I'm meditating?' Soon you realise you're thinking about last night's TV, your boyfriend (or girlfriend) or what you have to do tomorrow, and the breath is nowhere in sight! These thoughts stimulate you so you no longer relax.

It's so easy to slip back into automatic thinking, but once you notice that's happened, you've got the choice. If you let the thought go quickly, you are free. You might have to do this dozens of times before the mind adjusts to being in the present. This is the spade work of meditating. As you calm down, it becomes easier to stay focused. You'll still be aware of thoughts and sensations calling for your attention, but you will no longer engage in dialogue with them.

It's reassuring to know that everyone gets distracted when they meditate. I've been meditating for thirty-three years and I still lose my focus. Your skill as a meditator comes from being able to abandon a distraction fast. You spend a second rather than a minute with it. You cannot avoid noticing the thoughts, but you can learn to let them go rapidly. If you do this, they don't have time to stir you up. In fact, even the intention to let thoughts go is enough to let you relax.

... other thoughts and sensations

FOCUSING IS PLEASURABLE

Focusing is about directing your attention where you want it to go. It is the opposite of letting the mind ramble. It's a natural skill, and we cannot really achieve anything without it. You could not do the shopping or clean the house without paying some attention to what you're doing. Meditation just improves this skill.

The ability to focus is more important than the object you focus on. People commonly meditate on the breath or the body, but you could also focus on an activity, such as swimming, yoga, dancing or craft work; or an image, such as a flower or the ocean; or a mood, such as peace or relaxation; or a concept, such as God or emptiness. All that matters is that you choose a meditation object, and return to it when you get distracted.

Although it takes some effort to stay focused, it's a very satisfying thing to do. For example, if you eat a peach while thinking of other things, you barely taste it at all. If you focus on what you're doing, however, your pleasure is magnified. You feel your teeth breaking the skin, the juice on your tongue and saliva flowing. You notice the freshness, the mixture of taste and smell, and even hear the sounds of eating. The past and future, with all their concerns, vanish as you enter the small universe of the peach.

Focusing is enjoyable. It occurs naturally when something attracts us – a cloudscape, a flowering bush, a beautiful body walking by. A child absorbed in a toy is focused, sensing and present. Good focus is like focusing a camera: it catches fine detail. It magnifies the object in the foreground and dims out other thoughts and sensations in the background.

We cannot force the mind to focus, but we can gently encourage it. If we do this, eventually the mind will want to focus because the results are so satisfying: the mind feels clear, awake and in control, and the body becomes delightfully still. This doesn't happen if you just daydream or space out. And it certainly doesn't happen if you follow your thoughts.

How quickly and deeply you relax depends on how well you focus. It's as simple as that. You cannot help noticing other thoughts and sensations, but the more skilled you become at letting them go, the deeper you relax. When you understand this, you'll find you can focus on virtually anything in the world around you and relax whenever you want to. I'll give you plenty of possibilities to play with in the coming chapters.

7. Sitting comfortably

WHATEVER YOU DO – eating, walking or talking – you can be tense or relaxed about it. Just sitting in a chair, you could be far more tense than you need to be. Fortunately, if you notice how you are sitting you can relax markedly within seconds by adjusting your posture and freeing up your breathing. Furthermore, you can do this secretly while you are at a meeting or lecture, or on public transport. You can escape inside yourself, and no one notices you're gone.

We often assume we're relaxed when we're not. Sitting requires a certain amount of muscle tension to keep us upright, but we typically overdo it. Your body could be quite rigid even while doing something relatively stress-free, such as watching TV, sitting in a cafe or working at a computer. It all depends on your emotional state. If you're habitually anxious, some of your muscles may never relax, even in the deepest stages of sleep.

Tight muscles distort the natural balance of our bodies. The sitting posture of anxious people tends to be asymmetrical and angular. They typically tie themselves into defensive knots, and are 'on edge'. They don't let go and relax into the chair. They also forget to breathe.

When we're stressed, our first instinct is to blame our surroundings. Occasionally a student in my classes will complain that all the chairs in the room (and I offer a variety of models) are uncomfortable. In fact, it is their bodies that are uncomfortable, not the chairs. Don't believe those advertisements for expensive, multi-adjustable easy chairs that promise heavenly bliss. If you're anxious, your body will be uncomfortable no matter how 'comfortable' the chair.

HOW TO SIT COMFORTABLY

Years ago I did a Feldenkrais course on good sitting. I found it very illuminating but rather impractical. You cannot focus on sitting all the time you sit, any more than you can focus on breathing all day long. But you can deliberately relax when you need to, by making your posture more open and 'sitting comfortably'.

The first three exercises in this book all asked you to focus on the breath. In the next meditation you focus instead on your posture, but you still use the breath as an ally. You scan your body for unnecessary tensions and gently 'breathe through' them until they start to relax. They don't have to relax completely. It's quite enough if you just get the process started.

I suggest you move systematically through your whole body – adjusting this, letting go of that. Be slow and deliberate. Go right into a tension, whether it's in your neck, belly or toes, until you feel it starting to soften. Within two or three minutes you'll be sitting and breathing more easily and feel more centred in yourself. This is a really useful exercise, which you can do as a preliminary to any longer meditation.

Sitting Comfortably

Without changing posture, notice how you are sitting.

Ask: 'Am I more tense than I need to be?'
You may feel the tension in the face, shoulders or toes.

Also notice how you are breathing.

Adjust your posture, slowly and deliberately.

Sit straighter, loosen your shoulders, arms, stomach ...

Loosen up your breathing with a few sighs.

Go for balance, openness and comfort.

Now do the fine tuning, using the breath as an ally.

Go to the points of tension – face, shoulders, stomach – and gently 'breathe through' them. If you want, you can say an affirmation as you do so: 'let go', or 'relax' or 'peace'.

Don't expect the muscles to relax completely. Just feel them starting to loosen, then move on.

Do this for as long as you like.

Finally resume what you were doing, remaining aware of your posture and breathing as long as possible.

8. Scanning the body

THERE ARE HUNDREDS of practices based on the body and the play of sensations within it. For example, you can simply relax the muscles systematically from top to bottom. In yoga, you also focus on subtle energy flows and 'breathe through' blocks in the body. In t'ai chi and chi kung, you focus on moving the body in a fluid, harmonious way.

One of the oldest Western meditation exercises, dating back to the 1930s, is called progressive muscle relaxation. In this exercise, you tense and relax each part of the body in turn – toes, ankles, calves, thighs, and so on – from the bottom to the top.

It might seem as though you are 'making the body relax', but in fact something more useful is happening. You are learning to recognise how muscles feel when they are tense, and how they feel when they are relaxed. Ultimately, this awareness is all you need. When your mind knows what relaxed muscles feel like, the body will gravitate towards that feeling whenever you give it the chance.

In the following exercises, you **scan** the body in deliberate stages, from top to bottom or bottom to top. Focusing on the sensations in each place tends to make you aware of tensions, and this alleviates many of them within seconds. Scanning the body is like gently combing the knots out of a tangle of long hair.

As a result, you no longer need to do the hard labour of tensing and relaxing everything in turn. The awareness acts like the touch of a magic wand. It is quite enough to recognise that a muscle is tight for it to start releasing.

THE EFFECT OF SCANNING

Relaxation is a very physical process and, when you scan the body, you get to know it in detail. At first, the breathing loosens and the pressures of the day drop from your face and shoulders. The muscles soften and the limbs feel heavy. The deeper tensions come to the surface and gradually loosen their grip. In time, you come to know how each individual part of the body feels as it relaxes.

Many of the sensations you experience are quite subtle. The breathing eventually becomes very light, and the improved blood circulation gives you a sense of warmth and flow inside. The 'energy field' (that is, the network of sensations in the body) becomes more fluid and alive. It seems as if you're nourishing all the cells of your body by just paying attention to them.

Your perception of your body can change markedly when you relax. For example, when you are tense, your body feels somewhat solid and hard. As you relax, however, it feels softer and more fluid. At the edge of sleep, you may perceive the body in an almost dreamlike fashion as being numb or empty or barely there at all. If you notice these changes your meditation is clearly working well and you're doing the right things to make it happen.

YOU CAN SCAN QUICKLY OR SLOWLY

In the Countdown Meditation that follows (*see page 40*), you scan the body over seven breaths. You divide the body into seven regions from top to bottom, and breathe through each region in turn. This exercise only takes a minute, and is as efficient and portable as the Three Sighs meditation (*see page 10*). You can do it a dozen times a day, if you want to. It's easy to do even in, say, a supermarket queue, or while waiting at the red lights.

If you have more time available you can simply scan more slowly. Once you're familiar with the seven regions you will be able to spend longer in each one of them. Four breaths in each of the seven regions will give you a two-minute meditation. Ten breaths in each region can give you a five-minute meditation.

If you enjoy this kind of inner journey, let me encourage you to go even slower. Body scanning can have such extraordinary effects that I regard it as the most powerful of all healing meditations.

Many of my generation of meditators were taught to spend a whole hour doing one scan of the body from top to toe, or vice versa. You can feel the body in extraordinary detail if you try this, right down to the bones and organs. The body is alive with sensation: tingling, pulsing, pressure, pain, bliss, the ebb and flow of the breath. This inner music continually changes according to the activity of the mind and the depth of the meditation.

Body scanning illuminates the body from within. Although this can enhance our discomforts, it's also the royal road to bliss. It still surprises me that deep pleasure can coexist with the inevitable discomforts of having a body – even one that is in severe pain or gravely ill, according to some of my students.

As you scan, you can feel every part of your body, and all the systems within it, returning to a state of health and balance. Beneath the mild discomforts, the body can feel tranquil, radiant and vital. Because focusing magnifies what you focus on, you realise how good it feels just to be alive and conscious. You don't need to do a hundred things and spend extravagantly in order to be happy. Just breathing through the body works so much better (and it's a lot less expensive!).

SCANNING IN SEVEN STAGES

The following meditations ask you to scan your body in seven stages. The fast version, taking one breath to a region, is called the Countdown and takes less than a minute. The slow version, called the Body Scan, takes from two minutes to as long as you like.

Both meditations use a seven-stage template to give you a clear structure and something systematic to follow. For example, if you plan to spend ten breaths in each of those seven areas, you know exactly what you are doing for the next seventy breaths. This helps you stay on track and reminds you what to do if your mind drifts off into thought. Whenever this happens, simply pick up where you left off. If you last remember counting the third breath in the throat before you got distracted, that's where you get back on the train.

You'll also notice that the first minute of the instructions is an informal repeat of the meditations I've already given you. Whenever I use words such as 'sigh', 'breathe deeply' or 'sit comfortably', I am inviting you to briefly revisit what you learned in those meditations to set you up for the exercises ahead.

Countdown

Sigh *once or twice, and loosen up your posture.*
(You could be sitting, standing or walking.)

Now breathe through the body over seven slow breaths.
Each time you breathe out, move down one region.
Count on each out-breath as you do this:

'Seven' *– the scalp and forehead.*
'Six' *– the face.*

*'**Five**' – the neck and shoulders, arms and hands.*
*'**Four**' – the chest.*
*'**Three**' – the solar plexus.*
*'**Two**' – the belly.*
*'**One**' – the hips, legs and feet.*

*Now rest in one place, **breathing freely**.*
Or scan once again, as you wish.

Body Scan

Sit comfortably and shake your body loose.
Take a few deep breaths and sigh.
Scan your body at your own speed, noticing detail.
Count the breaths if you wish, spending four, or eight or ten breaths in each region.

Scalp and forehead
Notice tingling, pulsing, pressure . . .
Face and lower part of the head
Soften the eyes. Let the mouth and jaw go slack.
Neck, throat, shoulders, arms and hands
Like stroking or massaging the body with your mind.
Chest and upper back
Feel the lungs expand and contract.
Diaphragm and solar plexus
Feel the movement of the lower ribs.
Belly and lower back
Feel the soft organs move slightly as you breathe.
Hips, legs and feet
Feel or imagine the breath dropping through your body.

*Now rest in one place, **breathing freely**.*
Or scan once again, up or down, as you wish.

9. Coping with distractions

MEDITATION SEEMS SIMPLE ENOUGH – you're just trying to focus on one thing, such as the breath, and letting the other thoughts and sensations pass by in the background. So why is it so hard to stay on track? And why do so many people try to meditate and give up in disgust?

They get distracted, of course. The 'other thoughts and sensations' seem to be, and often are, more important than the meditation object itself. It's not surprising that they demand your attention. No matter how hard you focus, you still need to lightly monitor the background thoughts and sensations that stream continually through the mind.

When you meditate, you are bound to notice things other than the meditation object. Some of these things are sensory, like the sound of a barking dog, a cough or your shoulder feeling sore. Others are thoughts involving, for instance, thinking about what you are going to eat in the evening, or mulling over a TV programme you saw last night. Others still are moods or emotions: perhaps you are worried about your sick mother or delinquent son, or vaguely irritated by life itself. Some are memories of the past, or dream images. If you are trying to focus on the breath, you may feel most of these as unwanted distractions.

However, this 'mind stream' is not all negative. As you relax, it becomes more beautiful. You experience pleasant sensations and feelings, memories and insights, and these are definitely not distractions to be ignored. These are the very reasons why we meditate.

Yet meditation seems to trivialise it all by saying, 'Focus on one thing and let everything else pass by'. Does the breath really deserve more attention than everything else put together? Why on earth do we focus on it at all?

We do it because focusing slows us down. It keeps us from being swept away by the sheer volume and emotionality of our thoughts. It gives us a vantage point outside the mind stream, and enables us to watch it with detachment.

No matter how well you focus, you won't get rid of the mind stream altogether, and you don't need to. It's quite enough to notice those passing thoughts and sensations dispassionately. In fact, you often cannot relax at all until you do acknowledge them. That cocktail of thoughts, feelings and sensations is actually telling you where you're at and how you feel in that moment, and this is enormously useful. It's the basis of self-awareness.

So whenever you get distracted, don't be annoyed with yourself. Can you be a passive observer and simply acknowledge that particular thought or feeling? If you can, your mind is free, even if the thought remains. That's the ideal: a cool, dispassionate mind that reflects thoughts as if in a mirror, but doesn't engage them.

IDENTIFYING THE THOUGHTS

Once you realise you are giving a thought more attention than it deserves, you can disarm it by using a technique called Naming the Distraction. You simply ask 'What is this? What am I thinking about?' and 'name' it. You stick a label on it.

You 'name' the content of the thought: 'television ... food ... work ... money ... Sally ... James ...'. To do this, you have to stand back from the thought and see it from outside. It's still there, but you're not getting into a conversation with it. By naming it, you hold it at arm's length.

Naming the distraction serves to pigeon-hole it. The thoughts around 'work' or 'Sally' don't disappear, but you don't indulge them. They are still in the mind but not centre stage. You allow them a place in your consciousness, but only at the periphery, where they cannot dominate you.

Many people use imagery to help. They imagine putting the a thought on a shelf, filing it away, throwing it back into the mind stream or dumping it in a rubbish bin, depending on how important the thought is. These are all ways of lightly acknowledging the passing thoughts and sensations without being caught in them.

You can use very general words when you name your thoughts, such as 'distraction', 'past' or 'future'. Or you can be more precise and name the content of a thought, calling it 'money', for example, or name the emotion behind it (example: 'worry'). You can even name sensory things that are disturbing you, for instance 'barking dog', 'itchy nose', 'sore feet'.

... naming distractions

Naming often dispels a distraction rapidly, but that is not its sole purpose. In that split second, you're also registering what the thought is and how important it is. This is useful to know, whether the thought distracts you or not. Ticking off the thoughts and sensations as they arise has an organising function. It sorts them out and puts them in their places. In other words, noticing distractions is not a distraction in itself. It actually helps you relax and get your mind clear.

Whenever you are entangled in thought, you cannot relax. This can make you hate your thoughts and want to get rid of them, but this is a rather futile ambition. It's much better to aim for the middle ground: focusing on the breath while passively monitoring the mind stream.

Watching the stream of consciousness is a meditation practice in itself. It's called Vipassana, or 'awareness' or 'mindfulness', and it's developed most systematically in Burma. The exercise below, however, is not so much a meditation in itself as a strategy that you can use whenever you get distracted. If you lose your focus repeatedly, don't be annoyed with yourself. Simply pause and spend a second or two in identifying what you are thinking about. This is a useful thing to do and can be an integral part of any meditation.

Naming the Distractions

Relax the body and breathing as usual (see page 39).

Focus on the breath or on any meditation object.

Let other thoughts and sensations come and go in the background.

When you get distracted and lose contact
with the breath, don't be annoyed.
Just ask 'What is this?' or 'What am I thinking about?'
Don't rush. Let the object become clear and 'name' it:
It may be a sensory thing: 'pain … traffic … cold …'

Or a thought: 'work … money … holiday …'

Or a feeling: 'sleepy … restless … sad …'

You could imagine putting the distraction on a shelf,
throwing it in a stream or a rubbish bin,
or simply putting it in the periphery of your mind.

Don't analyse the distraction or try to get rid of it.
Just tolerate its presence.

Refocus on the breath as quickly as you can, and let the other
thoughts and sensations come and go in the background.

10. Walking meditations
part one

YOU CAN MEDITATE ON virtually anything while you walk, but in this chapter I invite you to focus inwardly on your body. In Chapter 20 I'll explain how to meditate outwardly on the sights and sounds around you. First, let me explain why walking meditations are so good.

When you are tense, your body is wired up for fight or flight. The most natural release, therefore, is to be active: to run away, beat up someone or scream. That's what the body wants to do. I can guarantee that doing this can make you feel good, temporarily at least.

Of course, there are less anti-social ways to burn off energy. People let off steam by fussing around the house, doing exercise or raving to a friend, and a few minutes later they really do feel better. They may not realise why, but their neck and shoulder muscles really have loosened, their breathing is easier and the stress response has faded somewhat.

Another way to destress, however, is to walk. If you wanted to, you could meditate every single time you walk, if only across the courtyard or to the car park. That could give you ten or twenty opportunities each day to burn off the stress hormones, and it wouldn't take any extra time at all.

The body enjoys moving. Walking is rhythmic and anything rhythmic has a slightly hypnotic effect on the mind. Walking moves the juices along and the keeps muscles and brain alive. It puts you in touch with yourself, your body and the world around you.

If you do walking meditations regularly, you could reverse the physical effects of a lifetime's stress. Habitually tight neck, shoulder and upper chest muscles lead to headaches, insomnia, pain, exhaustion and mental dullness. As you walk, you'll inevitably notice how some parts of your breathing and walking mechanisms are underused or malfunctioning. The simplest way to correct them is to walk consciously and breathe deeply.

If you want the luxury of full rhythmic breathing, you have to let go of rigid muscles throughout the body. Your whole body needs to swing and flow with the breath. The breath, in fact, illuminates subtle tensions and helps to loosen them up. The movement of the body and the breath as you walk can massage the muscles made tight by too much sitting and thinking.

WALKING IS AN ANCIENT MEDITATION PRACTICE

Is walking a second-best meditation? Most meditators assume you have to sit to meditate, but walking is just as traditional a posture. The Indian holy men and women of old were not monks. The monasteries came later. They were pilgrims, 'wanderers' or 'homeless ones', who brushed the dust of city life from their feet and roamed all their lives. They developed walking as a deliberate practice to keep their meditation continuous during the day. Over time, the walking meditations became elaborate and formal, especially as these holy people adapted to a more sedentary, monastic lifestyle. They're still used extensively in the East today.

Yet I think that ordinary walking, like ordinary breathing, is best. It's also more versatile. You can meditate any time you are on your feet – for instance while shopping, or while walking through a park, in a crowded street or even across a room. Since you cannot do much else while you walk, why not use it as an opportunity to relax?

SITTING MEDITATION IS NOT ALWAYS BEST

There are many reasons why sitting to meditate just doesn't work for many people, for example:

1. It can lead to excessive introspection and a desire to retreat from the world. In particular, it may not be good for depressed people, who are often lethargic anyway.
2. If you sit to meditate, all your worries can pounce on you. Once you close your eyes you may find yourself caught in thought from start to finish. It could be much easier to relax by taking a dawn stroll by the river or an evening ramble through the back streets.
3. We talk about the stress response leading to fight or flight, but there's another possibility: you freeze up. It's the stunned mullet effect. A sitting meditation may not work at all because, for some people, the muscles can remain locked in place. There is a kind of calm that occurs when you hold yourself rigid and immobile, but it's a false calm.
4. If we think of meditation as the deep, tranquil state that we only achieve while sitting, then we cannot integrate it into our lives. Our physiology changes when we move. This doesn't mean we're stressed, but the feeling is not like the low metabolic state we're in while sitting. Nonetheless, we can still be calm and clear-minded while active, even if it has a more awake quality.

SOFTENING THE EYES

Obviously, you need to walk with your eyes open, so you're bound to notice people, kerbs, cars, trees, sky, birds and so on. Your eyes usually hop from attraction to attraction like summer flies, but if they move too quickly, you won't be able to relax. There are, however, several ways in which you can settle them down. In all of them, your vision will be active enough to stop you bumping into strangers and tripping over kerbs.

1. You could hook your eyes on a point in the distance – like a car or tree – as if you were casting a fishing line,

and reel yourself towards it. This helps you resist glancing sideways. When you get too close, cast your eyes over something else.

2. Alternatively, look at the ground a few metres ahead. You can see perfectly well where you're going but not much else. (This makes you look quite serious and even pious!)
3. Or you can let your eyes glaze over slightly. Let them rest back in their sockets and half-close your lids. Try to evoke the way the eyes feel as you come out of a sitting meditation: soft and gentle and even a little out of focus.

The five meditations below all invite you to focus on the breath and/or the body in some way as you walk. Most of them simply adapt earlier meditations to the new posture of walking.

- *The first focuses on the sigh.*
- *The second focuses on deep breathing.*
- *The third focuses on breathing and scanning.*
- *The fourth counts the footsteps.*
- *The fifth synchronises breathing and footsteps.*

Walking Meditation
THREE SIGHS REVISITED

Sitting tends to restrict the breathing, but when you start to walk, you need more air. Therefore whenever you get up and start to walk somewhere for more than a few steps, sigh consciously three times to adjust the body to walking.

Whenever I get out of the house, the office or my car, I deliberately think: 'Breathe!' The big in-breath opens up the chest. The long sigh lets all the air go and softens the belly, and the pause at the end centres my mind in my body. If the out-breath is complete, I can feel the abdominal muscles continuing to soften and settle during the pause. It's delicious! In fact, a good sigh is an exquisite piece of artistry well worth cultivating. Here's the technique.

As soon as you start walking, think: 'Breathe!'

Take three deep sighs, enjoying each one fully:
the deep in-breath, the loose out-breath, and the pause.

Feel your ribcage opening up.

Move into the rhythm of walking.

Walking Meditation
BREATHING DEEPLY

Whenever you move from sitting to walking, your posture and breathing need to change radically. A whole array of different muscles comes into play and you need more energy (and therefore more oxygen) to use them.

So, as you walk, spend a good minute or so consciously adjusting your body to the requirements of walking. Your posture will become more upright and balanced. The in-breath opens up your ribcage and tends to lift the whole body, while a long, loose out-breath relaxes it.

Many people think of a deep breath as starting in the belly and moving through the diaphragm into the upper chest before going into reverse. If you want to relax deeply, however, it's much better to activate the diaphragm and belly, and ignore the upper chest.

So focus on pushing out the lower ribs and belly as you breathe in. Think of the breathing as happening horizontally (out and in), rather than vertically (up and down). If you do this correctly, you'll find your shoulders are barely rising and falling at all. This is a good way of checking if you're doing it right.

When you do a Deep Breathing meditation, I suggest you go for short bursts of high quality. Two to five minutes with your mind well focused will be much more relaxing than simply breathing deeply as you walk through a town. This is how you should do this exercise.

Sigh three times as soon as you start walking.

Let the sighs go, and simply breathe deeply.

As you breathe in, push your lower ribs forwards,
and as you breathe out, be sure not to slump.

Go for full, smooth and comfortable breathing.
Let the out-breath be as long as it wants to be.

Notice how quickly the breathing becomes tight again
if you let your mind wander off into thoughts.

Walking Meditation
WALKING COMFORTABLY

If we are anxious, we walk anxiously. You can see it in any city street. People walk with a stiff posture, hunched shoulders, tight breathing and worried eyes. Their bodies are knotted up by their thoughts, and burning a lot of unnecessary energy into the bargain.

Meditation is a simple antidote to all of this. An old Buddhist aphorism goes, 'When walking, just walk'. In other words, get out of your head and into your body. Let the past and future go, and focus on the sensations of the body moving.

If you pay attention to how you are walking, you'll soon walk more comfortably. Aim to walk with no excess tension. The body should feel balanced and open, with the hips and shoulders swinging easily. The breathing may synchronise with the footsteps.

Within a minute or two, you should be able to shift from tense walking to comfortable walking. The contrast can be very marked. Good walking has a beautiful, rhythmic swing to it, which is economical with your energy, and fluid in motion. Tense walking, on the other hand, is jerky and stiff, and takes a lot of unnecessary effort.

The difference is quite obvious, yet good walking is still vulnerable. As soon as your attention drifts back into your habitual thoughts, your muscles clamp up again and your breathing shrinks. Good walking demands that you consciously focus on, and stay in, the sensations of the present. This is what makes it a meditation.

Furthermore, even when walking comfortably you may find that some smaller muscles in your body are still holding on. This is because we never shift from tension to relaxation instantly – it always happens on a sliding scale. On a longer walk it is therefore good to systematically seek out those recalcitrant tensions and encourage them to let go.

If you focus for a minute on your hips, for example, I am sure you will find that they will start to move more fluidly. Then focus on your shoulders, and allow them to swing easily. Other common areas of persistent tension are the face, the upper chest, the belly and the feet. Spend half a minute or so on whatever part of the body calls for your attention, before moving on. In other words, casually scan your body as you walk.

***Sigh** three times as soon as you start walking.*

*Let the sighs go, and **breathe deeply**.*

*When your posture and breathing feel good, **scan your body**.*
Spend a minute or so freeing up your hips.
Do the same in your shoulders.
Feel your feet swinging easily.

Go to any tension that attracts you, no matter how small.

Enjoy the luxury of comfortable walking.

Be content to be present: when walking, just walk.

Walking Meditation
COUNTING THE STEPS

If you've burst out of the office at day's end with your mind in chaos, you'll need a very crude and obvious meditation object to focus on, or you'll lose it. In this case, count your footsteps. This meditation seems rather silly but it is an excellent emergency measure.

Since we can all count automatically, we need to make the counting more complex in order to stay with it. You walk at your usual pace but first count from one to five steps, then from one to six steps, then from one to seven and one to eight steps; then you go back and count from one to five steps again. The meditation therefore goes: '1, 2, 3, 4, 5! 1, 2, 3, 4, 5, 6! 1, 2, 3, 4, 5, 6, 7! 1, 2, 3, 4, 5, 6, 7, 8! '1, 2, 3, 4, 5!' and so on. You have to pay attention to do this, or you'll soon find you've counted up to 15.

Within a minute or two of focusing on this technique, you'll find you've stopped thinking about work (for example) and realised, 'It's quite a nice day out here!' You will have arrived in the present at last. Here's a summary of the technique:

Start counting your footsteps as you walk,
remembering not to lose count or go into automatic counting:
from one to five,
from one to six,
from one to seven,
and then from one to eight.

Repeat the sequence as many times as you like.

Walking Meditation
SYNCHRONISED BREATHING

In this meditation, you synchronise your breathing and footsteps, the way runners often do. You find out roughly how many steps you take as you breathe in, and roughly how many steps you take as you breathe out, and set that up as a pattern.

Mentally you count the steps. You may count three steps as you breathe in and four as you breathe out. Or you may have a two-three rhythm or a five-five rhythm. Just do what feels natural. If the rhythm changes as you continue to walk, then change the count.

The out-breath is usually a little longer than the in-breath. If it's not, you may be constricting your breath somewhat or not really relaxing at all. Remember that out-breaths that are short in comparison to the in-breaths are a sure sign of tension. Conversely, long out-breaths are a sign of relaxation. Try it out and see. A relaxed out-breath should have some of that timeless element of the sigh about it. If the out-breath is just a hiatus before the next gulping in-breath, you won't relax much at all. This is the technique:

*Start **walking comfortably**.*

Notice roughly how many steps you take as you breathe in, and how many steps you take as you breathe out.

Set that up as a pattern and count the steps:
'1, 2, 3' (on the in-breath), '1, 2, 3, 4' (on the out-breath),
or *2–3, 5–5 or whatever suits you.*

Change the pattern if you wish, as the walk progresses.

Enjoy the hypnotic tempo of this meditation.

11. Meditating at the Gym

IT MAY SEEM ODD, but a gym is a great place in which to meditate. I have a good friend, sixty-five years old, who was a Buddhist monk for many years. He is a profound meditator, so when his doctor suggested that he attend a gym to build his muscle tone, he found he would slip into a trance while on certain machines. Eyes closed, he would cycle into paradise, or sit motionless at the end of a set, much to the concern of the gym instructors who were training him. 'Are you all right?' they would ask, until they understood his eccentricities.

A gym is usually a noisy place. Amid the heaving bodies and clunking machines, there are often TVs and radios playing and conversations going on. So what makes it such a wonderful place to meditate in? Why do so many people (but not all!) feel relaxed in body and mind after a workout?

There are many meditations based on awareness of the breath and the body, but people often find it hard to focus on their bodies unless they're actually using them. Gym work puts you face to face with your body and gives you plenty to do with it. It makes focusing and being present that much easier.

Gym work is also relaxing because muscles need to be worked fully to relax fully. Underused muscles get stiff and painful, which is why a sedentary life, which might seem to be physically relaxing, actually leads to chronic tension and even disability in time. Gym work automatically gives hundreds of muscles within the body a chance to contract and relax fully.

Furthermore, the repetitive exercises you do in a gym can have a soothing, hypnotic effect. It's much more relaxing to do one thing again and again than to think about a dozen things simultaneously, as we're prone to do.

HAVING THE APPROPRIATE ATTITUDE AT THE GYM

Of course, many people talk to others, read magazines, watch TV or listen to the radio, think about their day or generally space out when they are at the gym. You couldn't say *they* are meditating. Neither are those who grunt and slog, striving to maximise their muscle tone and get a true 'gym body'; or those who go to the gym to discuss shares and property, or to pick up their next girlfriend or boyfriend. So what does a meditator do at the gym?

... to pick up their next girlfriend or boyfriend

Let me talk for myself. I don't go to the gym to achieve a perfectly toned body or to become an aerobics champion. I don't try to push the limits and be as good as I can possibly be. I don't pump myself up with positive visualisations to develop grit and determination. I certainly don't talk much to other people. Not at all. I go to enjoy myself and relax.

Years ago, I decided to make gym work a pleasure. I take my body to the gym the way you take a dog for a walk. You don't have to exercise your dog to the point of exhaustion each day, and neither do you have to push your body to the limits. All it wants is a bit of a romp. Muscles enjoy being worked and stretched regularly, and that's quite enough for me.

I know this approach works beautifully for me. Those moments when I'm totally attuned to myself and doing an exercise perfectly are so delicious they're almost ecstatic. Furthermore, I can feel my whole body saying, 'Thank you. I love this. It's exactly what I need.'

WORKING WITH WEIGHTS

At the gym I usually spend an equal amount of time on three different types of activity: aerobic work (walking machines, etc.), weight work and stretching (or yoga). In this chapter, I'll talk about working with weights; I'll discuss stretching in the next chapter.

Weight work, or 'pumping iron', usually consists of dozens of short exercises lasting a minute or two each. It therefore lends itself perfectly to doing one spot meditation after another. In a gym, there are dozens of machines that enable you to push or pull weights up or down or sideways, mostly with your arms or your legs. Each machine activates specific muscle groups such as the biceps, triceps or hamstrings, or regions like the lower back, shoulders or abdomen.

Usually you sit at a machine and push or pull a weight up and down as many times as you like. We can call each push or pull, a 'stroke', and people normally do a 'set' of ten or twenty strokes. So it is quite natural to make each set into a spot meditation of its own.

When you go to the gym, don't try to meditate for the whole hour or so that you are there. It's better to think that you have the opportunity to do maybe a hundred spot meditations in that hour, and then do as many as you like. Go for high quality in short bursts. Forty-five well-focused seconds are much better than vaguely trying to 'be present'.

Gym Meditation
STOP BEFORE YOU START

Your very first meditation is the Three Sighs. When you sit at a machine, make sure you arrive and centre yourself before you start working. When you sit down, you are quite likely to find that you are still holding your breath. This might be because of the strain of the previous exercise, or just due to the fact that you've walked a few metres across the room. Sigh consciously three or four times until you feel a good, long pause at the end of the breath. (By the way, this is a good exercise to do at the start of *any* activity.)

Sit down at a machine and let your body settle.

Take three or four deep breaths, and sigh.

Let the breath be completely loose, and wait for that pause between the breaths.

Feel that you've arrived and you are ready before you start.

Gym Meditation
COORDINATE BREATHING AND STROKES

Deep breathing is very satisfying, so don't forget to breathe just because pumping iron can be strenuous. People frequently hold their breaths or pant right through a set, and that's not relaxing at all. You can tell when people are doing this, because they usually let go with an explosive sigh afterwards.

So breathe as deeply as possible as you work. You actually need that oxygen in order to work well. Also, try to coordinate your breathing with your strokes. It's usually obvious how to do this, but some exercises automatically constrict the breathing because of the position or effort involved and so require some fiddling. The coordination can take some imagination, but don't give up on it.

Start the exercise, and coordinate the breaths and the strokes. (Notice that each exercise demands a certain type of breathing.)

Breathe fully and evenly, keeping the breath relaxed.

Try to match the end of the breath and the end of the stroke.

Gym Meditation
THE PERFECT STROKE

This is where the exercise becomes truly meditative. Here is what the Perfect Stroke should involve.

1. Can you perfectly coordinate the breath and the stroke? Do the in-breath or out-breath come at exactly the right time in the stroke? If they do, the action feels like a perfectly balanced inner dance between the body and the machine.
2. Is the stroke being carried out at the right speed? If you pump weights thoughtlessly, the movement tends to be fast and jerky. If the speed is just right, however, the action feels smooth and shapely. You'll find a light weight is better done more slowly, and a heavy weight more rapidly.
3. Is the stroke the right length? If you're working mindfully, you'll know the exact point at which you've pushed far enough. Beyond that, you over-reach and put some muscles under unnecessary strain. Furthermore the point of return occurs sooner towards the end of the set, as the muscles get tired.

Sitting at a machine holds your body relatively firm, so it's easy to isolate just the muscles you want to work. Using free weights requires more sensitivity in order to coordinate a larger range of muscles. In the search 2 the perfect stroke, you'll need to look harder for that inner stillness and a rhythmic interplay between muscles and breathing. It's quite an exercise to get it just right.

When you can say, 'That last stroke was perfect!' you are meditating. The breath was deep and perfectly coordinated, and the stroke was exactly the right length and speed. In that moment, you were undoubtedly 100 per cent present and in your body. It probably felt really good mentally as well. This is how to do this exercise:

First coordinate the breath and the stroke.

Now look for the one or two perfect strokes in that set.
Is the extension exactly right? Not too far or too short.
Is the speed exactly right?
Are the breath and the strokes exactly coordinated?

The perfect stroke will feel exquisite when you find it.

Gym Meditation
FOCUS ON THE ACTIVE MUSCLES

Now you can take it even further. This is where I suggest you close your eyes and 'place' your mind in the muscles used on that particular machine. You'll find there will be one exact location in the shoulders, arms, thighs or back that feels just right.

Imagine that you are 'breathing through' that place. If your breathing is smooth and even, the muscles will be working harmoniously. This means they're using just the right amount of energy for the exercise and no more. If you are pushing yourself or working mechanically with your mind elsewhere, it's quite easy to over-reach and strain yourself.

Close your eyes and place your mind in the active muscles.

Find the point of balance there and breathe through it.

Make the breathing gentle, full and focused.

Work the muscles without unnecessary strain.

Gym Meditation
FOCUS ON YOUR CENTRE OF GRAVITY

When you're doing an exercise well, you'll feel in touch with your whole body. It is a subtle feeling – harmonious, centred, strong – but you'll know when you've got it. Teachers of kung fu and t'ai chi say that all movement should originate from the *tantien* – the point in the belly that is your centre of gravity. A punch that comes from the belly is much stronger than one that comes simply from the shoulder.

So when you work a weight, try to feel a 'straight' line of energy from your centre of gravity through your body into the working muscles, and then into the weight. When you've got it, the core of your body feels perfectly still and strong throughout the whole stroke.

If you primarily focus on your centre of gravity rather than on the working muscles, your mind can be very still. That inner place deep in the body may not be moving at all, even though your arms or legs may be quite busy. When you work from that point of stillness, you'll also find there are no extra muscles getting into the act: you really do use just the muscles you need for that exercise.

Because pumping iron is strenuous, it's easy to lose that inner balance if your concentration wanders. When this happens, you'll over-reach yourself and feel strain. You'll also feel a wobble in that invisible line of energy from your centre of gravity to the working muscles.

Here's how to achieve and maintain focus on your centre of gravity:

Sigh two or three times and rest in the pauses.

Sink into your centre of gravity, somewhere in the belly.

Imagine you are breathing from this still, inner place.

Work the weights, keeping your attention in your centre.

Imagine a 'straight' energy flow from belly to muscles into the weights.

Notice if you start to strain or 'wobble': that's when you'll be losing the inner stillness.

Gym Meditation
STOP AT EXACTLY THE RIGHT TIME

People usually do sets of ten or twenty strokes on a certain machine, but this number is unlikely to be what the body really needs. The perfect point to stop could be after eight strokes or seventeen, on any particular day, depending on your energy levels.

You have to be well focused to catch that point. Your muscles will tell you when enough is enough if you listen to them. This can keep that enjoyable movement from degenerating into strain and tension. Letting your muscles decide when to stop a set is much more sympathetic than mechanically pumping out twenty strokes, just because that is what you always do.

As I said, I go to the gym to let my body play, as if I were taking a dog for a run. A dog will slow from running to walking, or will sit down and stop, at exactly the right time his body wants to. He likes to run but he also knows when to rest. He doesn't tell himself, as humans do, 'I'll stop running when I reach that tree in the distance.' If you let your body decide when to stop and start, and how much to do, you'll feel relaxed and energised when you walk out of the gym, rather than exhausted.

Breathe easily and do the strokes harmoniously.

Be as relaxed as possible while working the body fully.

Notice when you start straining and losing that relaxed feeling.

Wait for your body to tell you the exact time to stop.

Gym Meditation
PAUSE BETWEEN SETS

During a set, certain muscles and your breathing become tense. That's what toning the body actually involves. Pumping weights takes effort and oxygen, so you're likely to be breathing hard after a set, and certain muscles will have been pushed to their limits.

If you're not careful, those muscles can lock into place and stay tense after the exercise is over. We naturally rest between sets, and gym instructors may have told you that you need that rest to let the muscles soften. I see many people, however, holding on and not relaxing at all between sets. They spend their whole hour at the gym tightening each muscle group in turn and not allowing it to relax.

I suggest that you consciously rest between sets. Sigh deeply three or four times and don't start the next exercise until you feel the pause at the end. Even better, I suggest you 'breathe through' the muscles that you've just been working. Do this until you can feel them starting to soften. If the next exercise uses a different muscle group, they'll continue relaxing anyway.

When you stand up to shift to another machine, breathe.

While walking to the machine, take four deep breaths.

When you sit down again, sigh.

'Breathe through' the muscles you've just been working.

Wait for the pause between the breaths before you start exercising again.

12. Yoga and Stretching

MEDITATION HAS COME to the West largely from the traditions of Buddhism and yoga. Buddhism, however, as an old-time religion, is much more than meditation alone, while yoga is often just a form of physical fitness no more spiritual than weight-training. In fact, if you go to a local Buddhist group or yoga class you may learn virtually nothing about meditation, although the word is often bandied about to lend a certain 'spiritual' authority.

In yoga classes, 'meditation' often involves little more than doing breathing exercises or falling asleep on the floor at the end of a class. It can, however, be much more than this. Yoga has the potential to be one of the best possible combinations of physical exercise and mental training.

Yoga puts a high priority on stretching muscles and opening up the body. This makes it a perfect antidote to one of the major effects of stress: tight muscles. Adrenalin has the effect of tightening hundreds of muscles throughout the body, and yoga reverses this effect by stretching them through many ingenious poses.

Yoga is equally systematic in its use of the breath. Quite apart from its specific breath exercises, it emphasises full, deep, slow breathing while in the poses. This opens the muscles and joints to a degree that non-yogis cannot imagine. It also dismantles the habit of tight, upper chest breathing that is so characteristic of anxious people.

If you do yoga mechanically, it's just a physical exercise and nowhere near as useful as it might be. If your mind is anxious and tense, your body will be too, and your attempts to stretch the muscles will battle against the body's instinct to hold them in contraction. I've seen many anxious yogis trying to force their muscles to relax, and it just doesn't work.

Yoga becomes a meditation only when you consciously focus on what you are doing. The basic instructions for any meditation still apply: focus on a meditation object (in this case, your body), and let other thoughts pass by in the background. In other words, don't go on a mental ramble. If you pay attention to what you're doing, the yoga becomes much more satisfying and relaxes both the body and the mind.

The many poses are designed to stretch, and therefore relax, individual muscle groups in turn. This means that you focus on certain muscles and encourage them to let go as much as possible. Some poses, such as forward bends, are relatively passive, and the whole body can sink into the exercise. Others, such as the standing ones, are more complex and active, and involve some muscles tensing up while others relax.

So relaxation means at least two different things in yoga. Firstly, you relax certain muscles by persuading them to stretch out and let go. Secondly, when other muscles need to be tense, you tense them only to the degree necessary.

In fact, meditation is often described as a system of energy conservation: you use just the effort you need and no more. While some modern forms of yoga do involve high-energy sweat and strain, traditional yoga is usually more economical and more of an inner, mental discipline. The body is worked, systematically and gently, but you are training the mind to focus deeply as well.

It's your choice whether you do yoga (and indeed any kind of stretching) purely as a physical exercise or combine it with meditation. It's all a matter of where you place your mind. If you've read the previous chapter on meditating at the gym, you'll understand that the same general principles apply here: focus deep in the body, breathe consciously and monitor what you are doing. In fact, I derived those gym meditation exercises largely from the practice of yoga.

1. Breathe through the Stretch

Ease yourself into a pose and focus on the stretching muscles.

Notice the point of resistance in the stretch.

Place your mind there and breathe gently through it: use deep, full, slow breaths with a pause at the end of each.

Encourage the muscles to let go when they are ready.

2. Relax into the Pose

Settle into an active pose, for instance standing.

Notice that certain muscles need to remain tense.

Relax these muscles as much as possible, while retaining the pose: be economical with your energy.

Breathe deeply and slowly through the stretch.

3. Breathe Between Poses

Emerge from a pose deliberately.

If you are standing, expand your whole body. Stand tall.
If you are sitting, sit up straight and open the torso.

Breathe deeply and slowly, three or four times at least.

Wait for the pause between the breaths to be full and spacious before you move into the next pose.

PART TWO

THE SENSES

13. To relax, be sensual

THE PRINCIPLE IS QUITE STRAIGHTFORWARD: to relax, you simply have to 'be in the present'. You do this by focusing on sight, sound, smell, taste or touch. So far, I've asked you to focus mainly on the breath or the body – the sense of touch. In the chapters to come, we'll focus on the other senses as well. But first, let me explain why using the senses is so relaxing.

Right now, if you put down this book and listened *carefully* to the sounds around you for a minute, you would relax to some degree. I can guarantee it. You might hear traffic, birds, a distant conversation or radio, then a sound from next door. Soon, you would find your face and shoulders softening and your breathing slowing down. That's pretty good for one minute's effort. So why does listening to traffic have such a beneficial effect?

Listening is one of the five senses, and sensing pushes the habit of thinking into the background. Because excessive thinking is the fuel that powers the body's stress response, anything that reduces the fuel supply helps us to relax.

Sensing and thinking are in fact opposing functions. Sensing usually relaxes you and thinking arouses you, and one tends to eclipse the other. You simply cannot do a complex mathematical calculation, for example, and enjoy the flavour of a cake at the same time.

Sensing and thinking use different parts of the brain. Brain scans can tell which parts are being used because they require more glucose and get warmer. Some parts are activated when you process visual or auditory stimuli; other parts are used when you're thinking or talking. By consciously listening, looking or tasting, you divert your energy away from the thinking function. You temporarily starve those regions of oxygen and glucose.

Thinking and sensing even produce different electrical patterns. Thinking results in fast, erratic *beta* brainwaves, and sensing results in the slower, more rhythmic *alpha* brainwaves. Beta is a state of excitement or arousal, but even positive thoughts will stimulate you and eventually lead to fatigue. Alpha, on the other hand, is closer to your natural state of equilibrium. It's more restful and uses less energy.

Sensing slows down the overly active mind. Thinking is typically fast and jumpy: you might have a hundred thoughts and shifts of focus in a minute. When you are in sensing mode – listening to music or tasting food – your mind still moves, but much more slowly. Sounds and flavours tend to lure you inwards and invite you to stay.

... flavours tend to lure us inwards

Sensing is typically more passive and observant than thinking. To listen, you simply open the doors and windows of your mind and let sounds come to you. Sensing is like the listening or receptive phase of a good conversation. You're not actually 'doing' anything, but it is still a skill.

Sensing enables you to exactly notice the detail of a flavour, the subtlety of a colour, the location and quality of a sensation in the body. You only have to consider the abilities of a great musician, wine-taster or athlete to realise how much this skill can be developed – but just because we are all capable of listening or tasting doesn't mean we do it well.

BEING IN THE PRESENT

Sensing has the effect of bringing you into the present moment – the world of sight, sound, smell, taste and touch. It is amazing how little time we actually spend here – probably two or three minutes an hour on average. We live in our minds, and only check into the sense world for a second here and there to ensure that we don't bump into doors or get killed crossing the road.

The truth is that we're rarely here at all. Most of our mental activity is about what happened or what may happen. Both the past and the future are frustratingly uncertain and out of our control, and so give us little pleasure. As one old man said, 'I've had many worries in my life, most of which never happened.' Our hopes, fears, fantasies and interpretations can consume us.

Many people can see no way out of the endless inner dialogues, yet it is so easy to escape them. The prison door is wide open in front of them. They only have to step over that threshold and enter the present.

The world of the senses can be a lovely space, full of light and colour and beauty that we miss if we are lost in inner dialogue. This is the paradise that awaits us when we leave the past and future behind. It's right under our noses. We cannot live here and never think of other things. But we can walk into it whenever we like.

Do you want to be happier? Just spend more time in the present. Be more sensual. Five minutes more each hour would provide a huge improvement for most people. The intellect has its charms, but the sense world is where you find pleasure. To enhance your sense of well-being, I suggest you consciously taste, smell, see, hear and touch things every day. Regard it as part of your health-management and anti-anxiety regimen.

SENSING IS SIMPLER THAN THINKING

Paradoxically, meditation, or the art of consciously being in the present, is hard to understand because it is so simple. I've taught it to five-year-old kids and they get it without difficulty. Even teenagers do better than most adults. As mature, intelligent adults, however, we are used to thinking in complex and elaborate ways. We often juggle multiple trains of thought at once, and are modestly proud of our ability to do so. Meditation seems too simple to actually work.

Adults tend to think, 'Yes, I know how to relax. I've just got to focus on the sense world and let thoughts go.' They forget that understanding alone is not enough. Meditation, like any skill, needs to be practised to bear fruit. Or they think, 'Is that all there is to it? I must have missed something.'

We usually feel we have to 'do' something to achieve anything at all. Meditating, however, is a skilful kind of 'non-doing', and requires a deliberate passivity of mind. Meditating and sensing naturally take us back to a more childlike state of 'being' rather than 'doing'. The less you try to do, the better it works. The body and mind are able to return to balance precisely because you are doing so little.

This concept can be a little difficult to grasp. Of all the good lifestyle things we do for ourselves – exercise, good eating, social connections – this is the only one that emphasises non-doing rather than doing.

Of course, doing nothing is almost impossible for such a lively organ as the mind, so you go to the next best alternative. You do something simple and undemanding: you just listen to sounds, feel the breath rise and fall or look at something beautiful. Whether you look at a flower, taste a peach or listen to music, the effect is much the same. It brings you into the present, conserves energy, and slows down the body and mind. Meditation is about doing a simple thing, but doing it well.

14. FOOD AND DRINK

WHY DO WE LOVE EATING so much, even to the detriment of our health? It's often the most sensual activity of the day. The very act of eating – biting, chewing, tasting – pulls us into the present. It is an earthy activity that has more in common with animal functions than the sophistications of the intellect. It is not surprising that Christianity regarded Greed as one of the seven deadly sins. When you're absorbed in food, you're unlikely to be thinking about other things. Eating relaxes us because it temporarily eclipses the problems of the day.

Non-meditators usually think of meditation as a somewhat bloodless, 'spiritual' activity. The truth is that good meditators are more sensual and earthy than people who live in their heads. By spending more time in the present, meditators are literally 'embodied'. They feel their bodies from inside, with all their pleasure and pain receptors. Their sensory intakes – sight, sound, smell, taste and touch – are more vivid and satisfying.

Because sensing eclipses thinking, the fastest way to distract yourself from thought is to focus on something sensual. Food will do very nicely for this purpose. You could try to meditate for the whole twenty minutes in which you eat a meal, but that would be difficult to sustain. Instead, I suggest that you 'spot meditate' on food: go for short bursts of high intensity.

An old Zen story illustrates this kind of focus. A man is pursued over a cliff by a tiger. He hangs on to the root of a tree, but below him he can see yet another tiger waiting for him. Then he realises that the root is giving way and that he will soon fall. At that moment, he sees a wild strawberry hanging within reach. He plucks it and slowly eats it. It is the last strawberry he will ever eat, and his final comment is, 'How sweet it tastes!'

There is a similar story from the Desert Fathers of fourth-century Egypt, who were famous for their habits of fasting. One Father nonetheless had an annual request. As each fruit came into season, he would ask for a single specimen. That would be the only fig or pomegranate he would eat all year. You can be sure he enjoyed it.

There is a famous modern exercise designed to illustrate this kind of focus. It has now been flogged to death in workshops throughout the world, but it still works, and it involves a raisin.

The participants are each given a single raisin but, instead of gobbling it down automatically, they are asked to meditate deeply on the experience. First, they spend a minute looking at it, feeling and smelling it. They then place it in their mouths, and explore its texture with their tongues. When they finally bite into it, the rush of flavour and saliva can seem almost orgiastic. They continue to chew slowly and indulgently, refraining from swallowing till the last moment.

This kind of sustained focus has the effect of slowing down time and enhancing sensory detail. It acts as a magnifying glass. People commonly say with pleasure and amazement, 'I've never tasted a raisin like that before.' When the exercise is over, they also notice that their minds are calm and clear.

It seems crazy, but one way to escape all the problems in the world is to focus on a raisin. You won't escape for ever, but even a minute's respite can relax you enormously. Ten or twenty such minutes during the day could save you from a heart attack, a relationship break-up or a gambling addiction.

If you're doing something enjoyable, it makes sense to focus deeply on it. Anything that gives you pleasure is also likely to relax you. There is nothing like a cuddle or even a smile to soften a tense body. Try it out and test your blood pressure afterwards!

I've also found that good meditators rarely overeat. Years ago, when I'd finished a term of teaching, I used to book out a friend's vegetarian restaurant and take maybe sixty or eighty people there for a meal. It operated as a smorgasbord, and my friend said he would always prepare less food than usual when he knew we were coming.

His usual customers would tend to gobble down their food without really tasting it, and then go back for more. My students however, tended to eat more slowly and enjoy the food in front of them. Being more aware, they knew when they'd had enough, so they didn't overeat. This may also explain why meditators tend to be healthier and live longer than non-meditators: they're more inclined to eat the right quantities of the right food.

I often meditate on food or drink when I'm eating in company. If, at a cafe or a dinner, I find that my head is spinning with the buzz of the conversation, I deliberately withdraw into myself for a minute or two. I don't want to be any more reclusive than I am already, so I meditate on the spot. Without drawing attention to myself, I take a sip of coffee or a bite of food. That's the whole meditation, but it can seem to take a long time.

It goes something like this: first, I take a deep breath or two and adjust my posture. Then I slowly reach out my hand, feel it make contact with the cup and then feel the muscles tense to raise it to my lips. I consciously smell the aroma, tilt the cup, and feel the froth and the liquid coming through my lips.

I move the coffee around in my mouth, and feel my salivary glands respond and swallow. Then I deliberately put the cup down, noticing the very moment my hand separates from the cup. I relish the mental space this activity has given me, and when ready return to the conversation. The full technique is as follows – the instructions tell you what to do in the case of drink, but they can be adapted equally well to food.

Food or Drink Meditation

Take a ***deep breath*** *or two and* ***sit comfortably****.*

Mentally prepare yourself for the coming action.
Can you do it with perfect efficiency and grace?

Reach out your hand deliberately.

Pick up the cup and raise it to your lips.

Pause. Look. Smell.

Now tilt the cup and feel the liquid flow into your mouth.

Enjoy the pure luxury of it.

When you're ready, swallow.

Slowly return the cup to the saucer.

Feel the very moment the activity ends.

Notice how still your mind has become.

15. Just listening, nothing more than that

BACKGROUND NOISE IS an inescapable part of any meditation. Like the breath and the body, it is always with us. Any time we meditate, we'll inevitably be aware of sounds as well: the traffic, the air-conditioning, a dog barking, a car-alarm going off, a door slamming nearby, a plane overhead and so on.

We may occasionally be oblivious to noise but it's impossible to block it out completely. If you feel that silence is essential for inner peace, you set yourself an unattainable ideal. It's much better to accept the soundscape as it is, and even use it to meditate on.

You'll find that focusing on random sounds will make your mind sharp. You have to be alert or you'll miss the next sound. Although the sounds are unimportant in themselves, when you're totally with a bird call or a car horn, the past and future vanish. When you start to notice the subtle sounds you'd normally miss, you know you've arrived in the present.

Meditating on sounds can have quite a unique effect: it gives us a sense of space. Meditations such as the Body Scan (*see page 39*) have an introspective, inward quality that can make us assume we have to withdraw from the world to relax at all. Sounds, on the other hand, take us outwards. We may be focusing on things that are hundreds of metres away, and the mind expands to encompass them. We also realise we can relax while being fully conscious of our environment.

Random sounds give us a sense of space in other ways too. We hear one sound to the left and another far behind, and we notice the space between them. When a sound disappears, you find yourself gazing into space. The same happens if it is silent and you're waiting for the next sound. You can be totally alert, though focused on nothing.

Soon you realise this background space and emptiness is very stable. When people talk about an empty mind, this is what they mean. It's not a mental blankness, since you'll notice the next sound immediately. In fact, this space is the pure consciousness through which all our thoughts and sensations pass. Focusing on sounds can give you your first real taste of this.

Listening to sounds has another, more subtle, effect: it tells you what mood you're in. If you are in a bad mood, you'll project that on to the sounds around you and usually find them irritating and unpleasant. A minute or two later, as you relax, you may find those same sounds quite tolerable and even pleasant.

Listening to sounds is perhaps the most passive exercise in this book. It takes much less energy than deep breathing or walking, for example, but it still requires a little effort to do well.

A sound meditation is like that stage in a conversation where you're listening rather than talking. Often we're not very present during a conversation. Instead of listening to the other person talk, we commonly carry on our inner dialogues until it's our turn to speak again. We can be virtually deaf to what the other person says. A good doctor or counsellor, on the other hand, knows how to listen well. His mind is calm and attentive, enabling him to catch the important detail of what the patient is saying.

This meditation is ideal if you are at a meeting where you don't have to do much, but you still need to act as if you are there. If you go too deeply into a breath meditation, for example, you may be caught flat-footed when someone directs a comment at you. If you are listening to sounds, however, you'll know where the conversation is going and will be ready to respond if necessary.

Similarly, people often meditate in their offices or workspaces by doing a listening meditation. This alerts them to footsteps in the corridor or movement at the door. Or, if you're on public transport and your eyes are closed, the sounds will tell you when your stop has arrived.

Short meditations can be very powerful. A student told me that one morning at work had been so argumentative and frustrating, she was thinking about quitting her job. At lunchtime, she went in despair to a park and sat under a tree.

'I don't know how it happened,' she said. 'I listened to the sounds around me, and within a minute, I felt this deep peace come over me.' A few minutes later she went back to the office and breezed through the afternoon. Nothing had been resolved. In theory it was just as dreadful as it had been in the morning, but *she* had changed.

Random Sounds

Relax the body and the breathing as usual.

Tune into the soundscape.

Notice the background sounds you would normally ignore.

Don't reach after sounds. Let them come to you from all directions, and follow them to the point where they vanish. Try to catch a new sound the moment it arises.
Enjoy the textures and colours of sounds.
Listen to them as if they were music.
Enjoy the spaces between sounds.

Check your body to ensure you're actually relaxing.

Notice how simple this is: it's just listening.

16. Look at the world around you

YOU DON'T HAVE TO close your eyes to relax, though most people prefer it that way. I find it hard to convince people that open-eyed meditation is not just an inferior option. People commonly tell me, 'It never works with my eyes open.' They feel it's impossible to relax unless they shut the world out and fall into a torpor. There are many reasons why open-eyed meditation is good.

1. You can meditate anywhere, anytime – in a bank queue, a meeting or a waiting room, or while walking, exercising or doing housework – and no one notices. If, on the other hand, you have to close your eyes to meditate, your possible times and places are very limited. It remains something you can only do in private, like getting undressed or going to the toilet.
2. You can meditate on things of beauty. Flowers, candle flames and crystals are common things to look at. You could also focus on a tree, clouds, the wind in the grass, the colours of a sunset, a bird in the bushes, a painting, a dead leaf, a shadow, a spider web or the night sky.
3. Your meditation practice can become much more interesting. Meditating forever on the breath can get tedious. If meditation becomes a chore, you're unlikely to continue with it. Our minds do need to be entertained.
4. Being able to meditate on different things means you don't get dependent on one practice. Many groups and traditions want you to use only their technique, to bind you to them. They say things like, 'This mantra has a

superlative effect. Nothing compares with it.' But meditation is not about focusing on any one object. It is about focusing as a skill in itself. You should be able to shift your focus around, the way you direct the beam of a torch. You are learning how to direct your attention wherever you want it to go, both in the meditation and out, and that gives you great freedom.

5. Meditating with your eyes closed can make the mind a bit foggy, and that fogginess can continue for a few minutes afterwards. Open-eyed meditations, on the other hand, usually brighten the mind and make you more aware. A clear mind is like having clean spectacles, and this effect lingers after the meditation is over.

After meditating with their eyes open, people say things like: 'When I come in here after work I never notice the park. But when I leave, the trees look so alive and beautiful.'

... a bird in the bush

MEDITATING ON A VISUAL OBJECT

It is surprising how often we find beautiful things right in front of us – a flowering bush, storm clouds, a bright design on a dress or book, the grain of wood on a table. Otherwise, a spot on the carpet or someone's shoe will do just as well.

Although you're rarely likely to focus on something visual for more than two or three minutes, I'll give you plenty of options to play with. Don't feel you have to do everything. Just do what you want. The bottom line is: enjoy what you're looking at and relax.

I usually teach this meditation by putting several objects on a low table – some flowers, a candle, a mango, a piece of driftwood, a silk scarf. Some students are interested in none of these, and focus instead on the table or the carpet (which are also quite attractive).

You start by adjusting your posture and breathing for a few seconds. Then let your eyes roam over the objects till something grabs you. The next point is very important: you let your gaze soften into the object. If you stare rigidly, you won't relax.

When we are mentally active, our eyes move rapidly in their sockets. They move faster when we are tense and slower as we relax. It is not surprising that the eyes, and the little muscles that swivel the eyeballs, feel tired at the end of a day.

When you settle your eyes on one thing, however, they no longer need to move and the muscles around them can soften. You can let them relax almost to the point of being out of focus. When you do so, your whole face may soften in sympathy. Also, let the eyes blink as much as they need to.

Now gently observe colour, shape and texture. Let your eyes go for a lazy stroll over the object and highlight the photographic detail you didn't notice at first. In other words, you're not blankly staring in the hope that you'll relax. If someone asked you what your object looked like, you could tell them.

It's quite useful to 'name' your object, as they sometimes do in the East. In other words, you could say 'rose' each time you breathe out. Or if the colour is more interesting than the object itself, you could say 'red'. In fact you could do both, and say 'red' as you breathe in and 'rose' as you breathe out. This connects the breath and the object, and gives you more to hold on to. This is particularly good if you are in a place with many distractions, such as a supermarket queue.

You can also use your imagination, so long as you don't get too busy with it. Just as listening to music can evoke images, so can looking at an object. You can look at a flower and remember your grandmother had similar flowers in her garden. You can look at a mango and remember the taste and texture of the last mango you ate. You could look at a rock and imagine climbing it, as if it were a mountain. Or you see an elephant, or a face, in a design on the carpet.

It seems paradoxical, but you can often relax more rapidly with your eyes open than with them closed. A visual object can be much easier to focus on than the breath, so your mind is less inclined to wander. Within three or four minutes, you may have relaxed so much that your eyes want to close anyway. If they do, you'll realise how relaxed you've become. Although you may be mentally alert, your body could be virtually asleep.

You can even close your eyes and continue focusing on an object by going over it in your memory. Very few people see it vividly, as if it was projected on a screen, but we can all remember something about it. Just to say the words 'red rose' as you breathe would be quite enough to keep you focused.

Visual Object Meditation

Take a few deep breaths and let your body relax.

Now focus on something in front of you: the edge of a leaf, the letter 'T' on the title of a book, the pattern on a plate.

Increase the magnification. Use your mind like a zoom lens.

Slowly and playfully examine your object: see its colour, shape and texture.

Keep your eyes and your breathing soft.

Whenever you get distracted, gently return to the object.

Remain aware of your body,
to make sure you're actually relaxing.

Options:
Name the object, or colour, or both, as you breathe: 'leaf' or 'T' or 'pattern' or 'green leaf'.

Play with it in your imagination. What does it remind you of?

Close your eyes and go over it in your memory.

17. Where am I? Returning to the present

HAVE YOU EVER been driving somewhere, and realised you don't have a clue where you are? When you're caught in a train of thought, you can literally lose contact with reality. The exercise below brings you back to earth and the world of sight, sound, smell, taste and touch.

It still astonishes me how much this world differs from the world of the mind. It is more beautiful and vivid, and its pace is timeless and unhurried. It's like going back to the immediacy of childhood, but with the self-awareness of an adult.

For little children, the present moment is huge, while the past only started at breakfast time and the future stops at tomorrow. For adults, however, the past and future occupy most of our thoughts. We carry the disappointments of past years, and project our worries decades into the future. We go through the day with our minds elsewhere. It makes you wonder, 'Was it a mistake to grow up at all?'

Living in the past and future is bound to make us anxious and unsatisfied. The pleasures of the future are mostly paper pleasures, too fragile and unreliable to make you happy. Conversely, the pleasures of the moment are right beneath our fingertips.

The exercise below helps you reconnect with sight, sound, smell, taste and touch, and to rediscover the vibrancy of childhood. It works best if you deliberately slow down the speed of your mind and sink into detail, no matter how trivial it seems to be. Remember that thinking is usually fast and scattered, and sensing is a much slower activity.

Where am I?

Ask 'What am I seeing?'
What is in front of your eyes?
Sense the room with your peripheral vision.

Ask 'What am I hearing?'
In this very moment, what can you hear?
Explore the soundscape.
Check out the sounds from all directions.

Ask 'What am I touching?'
Notice points of contact: feet, buttocks, back, fingers and so on.
Feel the air on your skin.

Ask 'What am I smelling or tasting?' (If appropriate.)

Now sink deeply into any one detail. Enjoy it to the maximum.

Move slowly from sensation to sensation, as you wish,
staying with each one for at least ten seconds.

Feel your body relaxing as you do so.

18. Where am I at?

I'VE DESCRIBED 'BEING PRESENT' as noticing sight, sound, smell taste or touch, but this is an over-simplification. Our thoughts and feelings also happen in present time and it's good to notice what they are. Just because we're thinking doesn't mean we know what we're thinking about or how we feel. It's useful to occasionally see where we're really at.

In the exercise below, you simply notice how you feel, physically and mentally, from time to time. You check your body, your mood and your thoughts. To start with, you ask a simple question: 'Am I tense or relaxed, right now?' This usually makes you quite conscious of the unnecessary tensions in your body.

Then you ask yourself, 'What mood am I in?' (or 'What is my emotional state?'). This commonly draws a complete blank. We're just not used to noticing when we're sad or happy or worried or peaceful or angry or loving. We're much better at projecting a social facade of being 'okay', because that makes it easy to relate to others. Many people are quite anxious and miserable beneath their cheery exteriors.

If words seem inadequate to describe your state, you could ask, 'What do I feel like?' and seek out an image illustrating that. Images often encapsulate the feeling more completely than words like 'angry', 'sad' or 'excited'. For example, you might feel like a threadbare sheet, a hunted mouse, a squashed tin can or a bubbling fountain.

Finally, you ask yourself, 'What am I thinking?' I'm sure we've all had the experience of going through a working day with our mind elsewhere. You may be thinking about your girlfriend or your son, yesterday's argument, tomorrow's big decision, fears about money or a fantasy about winning the lottery. At any time, you may have several unrelated strands of thought going on, even if you're at a meeting or working on a computer.

These automatic thoughts are the ones that shape our moods and stimulate our bodies. Fortunately, you don't have to do anything about them, other than notice what they are. The principle in meditation is that passive awareness is enough. Once you become fully conscious of your bodily sensations, your emotional state and your habitual thoughts, then most of the work is done. As you see yourself in perspective, you'll find that most of the unnecessary tensions drop away fairly quickly.

Where am I at?

Ask 'Am I tense or relaxed?'
Since you'll probably be more tense than you need to be, relax your body and your breathing.

Ask 'What mood am I in?'
Find a word that captures that feeling: 'sad, restless, racy . . .'
Alternatively, ask 'What do I feel like?'
Find as graphic an image as possible.

Now ask 'What am I thinking about?' or 'What have I been thinking about today?
Watch patiently for a few seconds, and 'name' the subjects of your images as they appear: 'Miranda . . . John . . . work . . . money . . .'

Finally, survey your body, your emotions and your thoughts. This is you, right now. It's where you're at. Just accept it all. Notice how it all changes, without your having to do anything.

19. Snapshot: the Sensuality of Little Things

THIS IS POSSIBLY the shortest meditation in this book. In this practice, you go for maximum focus for a very short time – it's like taking a photograph. If you can deeply enjoy the sensuality of little things, they break up the greyness and gloom of a stressful day. The texture of a nectarine, the sound of squabbling birds, the cool morning air on your face, the smell of your lover's hair are all so much sweeter than your habitual thoughts.

If you look carefully at anything, you'll find you can bring it to mind later in the day. For example, I can still remember the little white chihuahua I saw as I walked to the supermarket this morning. If you cannot remember things such as people's names, it's usually because your mind was too preoccupied by other thoughts to notice them in the first place.

I love to meditate for short bursts on visual objects. I call this 'taking a snapshot'. I aim for a few seconds of total absorption in a leaf, a bird's feather, the bark on a tree or a shadow on a wall. The 'exposure' may only be five seconds, but it cuts the other thoughts dead. In those few moments, I've lost myself. I'm just leaf. I'm just chihuahua.

I often do this while walking. I pass a cat on a brick wall and imprint it in my mind. As I walk on I play over the memory of the cat for the next half minute or so. It is extraordinary how much detail you can catch in a flash.

At the end of the day, it is easy to bring one of those snapshots back and focus on it for a few seconds more. It is like reliving the loveliest moments of the day. In fact, I can still remember snapshots from years ago.

You don't have to confine yourself to visual objects. It's an interesting challenge to take 'snapshots' of sounds, smells, flavours and tactile sensations as well. Can you replay the taste of a nectarine, the texture of your cat's fur or the sound of a flock of birds flying overhead? It's good to do this systematically. Why don't you try to imprint ten beautiful sensations in your mind, tomorrow?

A similar practice is to give yourself colour cues to remind you to meditate. Decide that you'll take snapshots of all the blue or yellow things you see in a day. If you like to do visualisations, this is a good way to develop your ability to imagine colour.

Snapshot

When something attractive catches your eye, take a snapshot:
Give it your total attention for five seconds.
Imprint it in your mind.
For the next few seconds, examine the detail in your memory.

It doesn't matter if you think you're imagining things.
So long as you're totally focused, you'll relax.

A few hours later, take out the snapshot and look at it again.

20. WALKING MEDITATIONS
part two

WHEN WE ARE SITTING, we can get so absorbed in our thoughts that we barely notice the sense world around us. When walking, however, you cannot avoid noticing your physical environment, and this makes walking ideal for meditation. In Chapter 10, I explained how to focus inwardly on the breath and your body as you walk (*see page 50*). Here, I explain how to focus outwardly on the sights and sounds of the world around you.

The best way to integrate walking meditations into your life is to select some place where you walk regularly. The walk to the shops or the bus or the carpark will do nicely. A walk of about two to five minutes is perfect. Once you've meditated in

... some place where you walk regularly

a particular place a few times, it will act as a cue to remind you. Each time you enter that space, the thought will arise: 'I'm here again. Shall I meditate now?'

I often get up early and work, but by eight o'clock I'm ready for a break, so I go to collect the post from the post office. This involves a lovely walk through tree-lined streets and past attractive little houses. It only takes five minutes, so it's a wonderful opportunity to get out of my head and come back to earth. I've come to know all the trees and shrubs, and the little park on the way, extremely well over the years.

Walking Meditation
SOUNDS

Walking exposes you to far more sensory stimuli than sitting does, so you need to be quite selective about what you focus on. In this practice, you put sounds in the foreground and other sensations in the background. You choose to emphasise and magnify the sounds you hear, while giving minimal attention to the objects of other senses.

When you hear a sound, try to hold on to it for a few seconds at least.

Savour the texture of each sound.

If you skim too quickly from sound to sound, you'll soon skim back into thought. So actively focus and dwell on sounds, while passively noticing the other sensations. Take a snapshot of each interesting sound, if you want.

It's not that the other sensations are bad, or distractions that have to be avoided. It's just that deeper focus encourages the mind to slow down and settle.

Walking Meditation
VISUAL OBJECTS

When we walk, there are hundreds of visual objects that can catch our eyes. Our eyes usually scan at random, semi-consciously taking in the scene and looking out for danger. They typically flit around, not staying on any individual object for long.

To relax, however, I suggest you slow down and consciously look at things. It's much more enjoyable this way.

Let your eyes move as they wish from tree to sky to grass to footpath, but do it more slowly than you would normally.

Linger with each one for at least ten to fifteen seconds, until it really comes into focus and the fine detail becomes obvious.

Don't go looking for something new too quickly. Wait with one thing till something else grabs you. You could even return to the breath until something else arises. It's much better to look at ten or twenty things really well, than to look vaguely at everything.

Walking Meditation
WIND

This ancient practice is quite delicious.

Focus on the movement of air over your body as you walk or even sit outside. Even on a still day, the air masses shift around you, touching your cheek, neck or leg in succession.

This is a very sensual practice. It feels like the earth is breathing over you. It's quite passive, like listening to sounds. You just wait for the next lick of air on your skin.

Walking Meditation
BEING PRESENT

The earlier exercises invited you to focus primarily on one of the senses – sight, sound or touch. In this meditation, you combine them, and can even include the sense of smell as well.

Focus on whatever sensation catches your attention in the moment.

Shift your focus as you wish.

What makes this different from a stroll in the park is that you linger with each thing for at least ten seconds until something else replaces it. You sink into the detail: the smell of the earth, the sight of birds fighting, a blast of wind in your ear, the crunch of gravel underfoot. It's still a discipline. You notice when you're wandering back into thoughts, and return to the present.

Walking Meditations

Take three ***deep breaths*** *as you start to walk.*

When you feel you're ***walking comfortably****, focus.*
Listen to sounds.
Or *look at one visual object after another.*
Or *feel the wind move over your body.*
Or *be present, moving from one sensory input to another.*

Stay with each object or sensation for at least ten seconds.

Go into it and explore the detail, before moving on.

Keep a background awareness of your body.

21. AFFIRMATIONS: HOW WORDS CAN HELP

THERE ARE MANY WAYS to use words to keep you focused. You could count your breaths, or say the words 'in, out' as you breathe. You could name the object you are focused on, each time you breathe out: 'fire, fire, fire'; or you could name the activity: 'swimming, swimming, swimming'. These all have a slightly chant-like effect and help to keep the mind from wandering.

An affirmation is similar, except that it also contains some useful ideas. Meditation is ideally a 'thought-free' zone, but affirmations are in the middle ground between thinking and sensing. Since this often encourages thought, it can be both an advantage and a disadvantage, as I'll explain below.

Here are some affirmations:

- ***Peace***
- ***Relax***
- ***Slow down***
- ***Be here***
- ***Let go***
- ***Let it be***
- ***Love***
- ***I'm okay***

It is good to find your own affirmations. Any word or phrase that evokes a good feeling will do. If, for example, you enjoyed a recent holiday in Spain, you could use the word, 'Spain'. The name of an absent lover or grandchild, or a short phrase from a poem or a song, would work equally well.

Affirmations can set a mood quickly and can be like a mini-instruction, reminding you what you're trying to do. If you are getting uptight at work, just saying the words 'let go' a few times as you breathe could do the trick.

USING AN AFFIRMATION AS A CHANT

There are two very different ways of working with an affirmation. You can say it like a chant, or you can use it as a starting point for contemplation. The first will relax you more deeply, while the second can give you useful ideas.

Affirmations do involve words and concepts, but in a very simple form. Repeating a single word or short phrase hundreds of times tends to squeeze other thoughts into the periphery. Even though there is more intellectual content in an affirmation than in the breath, saying one word repeatedly will stop the mind from chattering on in the way it usually does.

Affirmations work well as a back-up to the breath or to the body-scanning meditations. This is like using them as sonic wallpaper or ambient music, rather than as a springboard for thought. It adds an encouraging mood, but it's not the main focus of the meditation.

So what kind of affirmation is best? A short or a long one? A simple one or a beautiful and spiritually uplifting one? Meditation works by streamlining your attention, so in general the simpler the practice, the deeper you go. If you want to be calm and relaxed, a short affirmation with a clear idea will work best.

AFFIRMATIONS FOR CONTEMPLATIVE THOUGHT

Affirmations are also used as a vehicle for thought or as a way of changing mood. In the Christian and New Age traditions, you relax and contemplate an inspiring idea, often with visualisations included. People will use affirmations to combat negative thoughts and reprogramme their behaviour, as a kind of direct cognitive therapy.

Attractive as this seems, people who try to evoke beautiful thoughts often fail to relax at all. When you pursue some thought with a goal in mind, there is bound to be some tension and effort involved, and the process may be much the same as normal thinking.

It's even worse if you regard an affirmation as an order from the mind to the body, because the body rarely responds to that kind of treatment. So don't forget to actually relax while you say your affirmation. Otherwise, your meditation will just be a head trip.

On the other hand, if you are deeply relaxed, an affirmation can trigger off a deeper, slower kind of thinking that is quite useful. The secret is to say the affirmation without actively thinking about it. It's usually best to crystallise the idea into a single word or phrase and say it silently to evoke the calming effect of a chant.

I suggest you simply hold the thought in mind and wait for any associations and insights to arise around it. At the edge of sleep, you may even start 'thinking' in imagery and feeling as well as in words. The goal is to deepen the mood in whatever way you can and wait for the feeling to arise.

So what do you want more of in your life? Peace? Love? Health? Happiness? Let's look at these. When you say 'Peace' you are effectively asking, 'What is peace?' and seeking the feeling. It's there. You know what it's like. You've been there before. You just have to keep your eyes on it, and not get distracted. Just saying the word repeatedly as you start to relax can allow the feeling to blossom.

When you say 'Happiness' you are also asking, 'What will make me happy?' both in this very moment and in the long run. Your body will eventually tell you what it wants, if you listen. You may find that hopeful fantasies about the future just make you more restless and dissatisfied. Happiness could be more accessible than that – a matter of coming into the present.

When you say 'Health' you are asking, 'What is health? Am I in a healthy state right now?' Physical tension is the most obvious sign of malaise in your body, and you may notice that your mental activity is causing that. By watching your body responses, you can see how your thoughts and actions are affecting your health.

'Love' is something we talk about a lot, but often in abstract terms. What does it actually feel like? A sense of warmth or flow or ease? A strain or a longing? Is it on the surface or mostly hidden? Does it come and go and sometimes get lost altogether? What is the feeling of being loving towards yourself? Do you feel love differently towards different people? I suggest you bring someone to mind and meditate on the feeling that arises within you when you do this.

If you meditate frequently on peace, happiness, health and love, you'll actually know what they mean to you. You'll know what your body feels about them. They won't just be concepts and you won't get trapped in the words you spin around them.

SETTING GOALS

Using affirmations to set goals is hardly what you do in five minutes, but I'd like to say something about it here. Positive thinking and creative visualisations are a very American way of meditating that go back to the 1800s; they stem from ideas such as the one that any poor immigrant can arrive at Manhattan Island and become a millionaire if he believes he can.

You set up an ideal and work towards it. You make your goals as real in your mind as you possibly can, reinforcing them with visualisations and affirmations. It's a kind of positive self-talk. You picture the ideal job, the ideal mate, where you want to be in five years' time and the steps along the way.

There is no doubt that many successful people operate this way. They don't blunder along hoping nice things will happen to them. They go into the supermarket of life with their shopping list written out. But this only works for a certain kind of person, and it is counter-productive for others.

The negative side of positive thinking is that you can live in fantasy and unrealistic expectations. Our thoughts don't create our reality: they only shape it somewhat. Having a dream and following it doesn't mean it's going to happen, no matter how much you believe or how beautiful the dream. If you live in fantasy and hope, you can get badly hurt when you're brought down to earth. And if your only strategy is to fantasise some more, you could get into a very delusionary state.

Goal-setting affirmations work best to reinforce something that is already happening, and to remind you what you are doing. They cannot materialise things out of thin air. To use a simple example, if you say the word 'peace' when you are in a state of panic, it probably won't work. But when you start to relax and the first traces of peace are visible, then the affirmation will strengthen them.

So, to summarise, if you want to relax deeply, use an affirmation in a chant-like, almost mindless way. If you want to contemplate an issue, it still helps to relax as deeply as you can first. Don't sacrifice your physical relaxation, which is so important to your well-being, just for the sake of an attractive fantasy.

Affirmations

Relax your body and your breathing.

Say an affirmation, and blend it with the natural breath.

If the breath is short, shorten the affirmation.
If it is long, stretch it out.

Enjoy the chant-like, slightly hypnotic quality of this.

Let the affirmation set a mood, like ambient music.

Focus more on the breath than on the words.

Contemplate the meaning of the affirmation if you wish.

What kind of feeling does the affirmation evoke in your body?

Allow images and associations to arise around the affirmation.

Don't get too mentally active. Stay in touch with the breath.

Make sure the body remains passive and open.

PART THREE

ACTIVITIES

22. Pay attention to what you are doing

AS I'VE MENTIONED BEFORE, you don't have to sit down with your eyes closed to meditate. This is just the first stage, and it's unfortunate that many experienced meditators never go beyond it. A much better goal is to be as relaxed and clear-minded as you can be throughout the day, and use every opportunity to return to balance.

Unfortunately, this ideal goes against the grain of our habitual behaviour. We tend to operate on automatic pilot. We can scramble through the day not sensing or feeling anything clearly. What is worse, we can be too distracted to realise it. Some days, we're just not here at all.

Operating on automatic pilot does give the mind a break, but so does heavy drinking and junk TV. Although it is restful, it blurs our perception of reality and so is a mixed blessing. Just because we wake up in the morning doesn't mean we are fully here. We can switch on the TV, read the paper and have something to eat, then move from one distraction to another all day.

However, we cannot genuinely relax when we are absent-minded or caught in our thoughts and diversions. We only relax in the present, not in the past or future. To help you be present, the Buddha suggested the following: 'When walking, just walk. When eating, just eat. Similarly when standing, sitting, getting dressed or going to the toilet.'

Our problem is that when walking, we think about work. At work, we think about sex. When with our lover or spouse, we think about last night's TV. When watching TV, we also eat, read the newspaper and talk to someone. It is not surprising that the mind gets confused and exhausted, and we feel stressed.

And we don't enjoy the TV, the food or the love-making as much as we could.

Buddhist psychology is somewhat puritanical, but it still makes good sense. The Buddha said, 'Awareness is the cure for suffering.' In other words, if you blunder through life in a daze, you'll frequently hurt yourself and be miserable. A more cheerful expression of that idea is: 'If you want to be happy, be present. Know what is happening as it happens.'

The Buddha gave systematic instructions to his monks and nuns on developing this moment-to-moment awareness. They are quite clear and it's easy to imagine following them, even though they're 2,500 years old. They go something like this:

At first, he said, meditate with your eyes closed, sitting under a tree. Then practise walking to and fro in front of your tree, realising that you don't have to be distracted by what you see. Then walk mindfully to the local village (walking meditation) to scrounge some food (standing meditation).

Of course, there are many temptations here to distract you. The hustle and bustle can be quite attractive after a long morning's meditation. A handsome man walks by or a beautiful young woman puts food in your bowl and reminds you of what you are missing. Even the simple life of a begging monk or nun can be full of turmoil.

Then you walk back to your tree, and do the eating meditation. Then the lying down and trying not to fall asleep meditation. Then you get up mindfully and rearrange your clothing. You walk to one side and urinate, listening to your urine fall on the dry forest leaves. In the texts, these are all described as conscious meditations, with clear starts and finishes. (I'll detail some of them in the coming chapters.)

Throughout the day, you meditate on your natural surroundings – on earth, water, fire, air, light and space in particular.

Similarly, you observe the cycles of sensation, thought and mood within your mind and body during the day.

THE NAMING TECHNIQUE

To enhance your awareness, you could use a technique called 'naming'. Each time you breathe out, you might 'name' the activity you are engaged in: 'walking, dressing, listening' or whatever. Or you could name an object that caught your attention: 'monkey, man, woman, food'. You could even name your internal state: 'peaceful, restless, sleepy'.

Naming helps you to develop that self-reflective, observant quality of mind that is called 'awareness' or 'mindfulness'. This means you are in the present: you know what you are doing and what you are thinking, as it's all happening. This awareness turns out to be remarkably useful. It cleans out the stress and mental rubbish, and is the foundation for all self-understanding and clear decision making.

MAKING SIMPLE ACTIVITIES INTO MEDITATIONS

Because being present seems like a good idea, you may decide that, 'Today I am going to live in the present!' However, it is better to be more modest with your goals. Don't try to be present for an hour or a day. Just try for a few seconds or minutes at a time. Aim for high quality and short duration.

It can be surprisingly satisfying. Try to eat a biscuit consciously. Enjoy watering your plants. Brush your teeth deliberately. Hang out the washing as if it was important to do it well.

Simple household tasks are excellent for bringing you into the present. It can be very satisfying to just potter around the house, cleaning, tidying, preparing food and so on. Many people find an almost primeval satisfaction in looking after the house and garden. The servants and artisans of the past did not earn much respect for their work, but many would have found a deep contentment in the humble rhythms of their lives. The medieval guilds understood the spiritual dimension of ordinary work, but we've mostly lost that idea nowadays.

It may seem to you that for your whole life long, you'll be doing mundane tasks like picking up socks, ironing shirts and washing dishes. If you feel such chores are something you have to get out of the way before you enjoy yourself, you'll constantly be tense and rushing from one thing to another. If you use them to relax, however, they can be a real pleasure.

... simple household tasks

The Zen tradition emphasises the remarkable possibilities of ordinary work. 'Chopping wood, and carrying water – miraculous activity', goes one Zen saying. Sweeping the courtyard is the subject of many Zen poems. Boiling rice, washing the vegetables and repairing your clothes in the candlelight are all described as opportunities for deep tranquillity.

The following chapters describe how you can focus on an activity such as housework, driving or gardening. Such activities can work well to keep you focused, because one little action automatically leads to another. You don't have to voluntarily direct your mind, since the activity itself can lead you along.

Some people find this kind of meditation so natural they barely need to practise it at all. They find gardening or craft work, for example, so engaging that just doing it relaxes them. Most of us, however, need to put in more effort. As a start, I suggest you select an activity that is relatively simple and pleasant, and then do it as a meditation several times over the next few days.

This sounds simple and obvious, but it's very easy to get sidetracked. Meditation is a modest and unassuming activity. It can easily get pushed aside by things that seem much more important or interesting, such as phone calls, Internet-surfing or reading the newspaper. If you're new to meditation, there's a tendency to put it very low on your list of priorities.

So, can you do the same meditation four times over four days? This won't cost you any time or money, but it does require some dedication. The pot plants need to be watered regularly to thrive. Unless you practise Being Present conscientiously, it will just remain an attractive idea that never quite takes root in your life.

23. Household meditations

YEARS AGO, I did a seven-month retreat, most of it in a tiny hut high on a mountainside in the Southern Alps of New Zealand. I was alone all week, except for Wednesday, when I collected my food for the days ahead. I did sitting meditations for about nine hours a day, plus three or four hours of yoga and walking meditations.

Inevitably, the housework became infused with the spirit of meditation. I particularly looked forward to preparing my food. That secluded lifestyle naturally enhanced sensory awareness, so making a meal became a little drama of sight and sound, smell and texture that I enjoyed enormously.

Nowadays, I will still do those 'kitchen sink' meditations while preparing food. Sometimes I focus on just one sense, such as sound. I deliberately listen to each sound I make: cutting the apple, putting the knife down, the squeal of the tap and the water running, the bowl scraping on the bench, a foot shuffle, the fridge door opening, the clang as I place something on a rack and so on. I am aware of other sensations of course, but I highlight the sounds.

I was trained to hold my mind to the task by saying the word 'sound' silently, each time I breathed out. I find this 'naming' technique works well to stave off distractions, particularly at the start of a meditation, or if the meditation is very short.

Alternatively, I notice input from any sense. The keyword for this is 'sensing'. Preparing food naturally moves your attention from sight to sound to texture to smell. It can be quite exciting! So I notice the texture of the knife, fruit, water, the door handle; or the glistening skin of a capsicum; or patterns of light and shadow; or a stain on the bench; or the sensations in my arm as I lift something or put it down.

I check myself non-verbally by asking, 'Where is my mind, right now?' It is amazing how rapidly my mind can disappear into thought, and how interesting the sense world can be if I focus on it.

HAVING A CUP OF TEA

A cup of tea is an excellent thing to meditate on. For myself, I find the actual making of the tea works better than the drinking of it. This is because making tea consists of many small, delicate movements that lead naturally from one to the other, with the occasional short pause between them. There are textures, smells, sounds and physical movements, all in the space of a few seconds.

Even better, making a cup of tea has a clear start and finish, so you know when the exercise starts and stops. It starts with the intention and finishes when you put the tea where you're about to drink it. It's an activity that doesn't just fade away into something else and, because it only takes two or three minutes, you can give it more complete attention than you would to a longer activity. As I say repeatedly through this book: high-quality focus for short duration is best.

Tea, in fact, has an ancient connection with meditation. It was such an essential ingredient in Tibetan monasteries that blocks of tea were used as a form of currency. The monks would continuously sip tea during the day. Clearly, it helped keep them warm in those drafty monasteries in winter, but I think it was equally valued for its caffeine content.

The altitude and the frigid climate in Tibet discourages activity and keeps people huddled inside small, poorly ventilated rooms for much of the year. The caffeine would counteract the resulting mental lethargy. On the practical side, it kept the monks awake during their marathon chanting ceremonies that often lasted for days.

A more elegant use of tea is the Japanese tea ceremony. This is a beautiful, multi-sensory meditation in which the making is just as important as the drinking. As the guest, you watch each movement of the tea-maker. You enjoy the decorations in the room, hear the sounds, watch the steam, feel and look at the bowl, taste the tea and feel yourself swallowing. You become calm by focusing on one small detail after another.

The ceremony is very formal, especially if it is held in a specially designed tea-house in a garden, and it encourages you to be fully present for the whole thirty minutes or so. It was cultivated in medieval times to create a tranquil space in a violent world. The samurai warrior caste for whom it was designed would symbolically leave their swords, and their warlike nature, outside the hut to enter that space.

You can do exactly the same in your own kitchen. If you want to escape the warfare of the modern world, turn your back on it and make a cup of tea.

TAKING A SHOWER

I did my first ten-day retreat in 1975, and I had an epiphany on the third day: I had a shower. I went into the shabby cubicle at the old Catholic retreat centre in Auckland, New Zealand, and had such a shower as I'd never had before in my life.

The meditation made my mind so still and clear that time slowed down, and every sense was heightened. When the water hit me, it was an explosion of delight – colour, texture, sound. I felt my skin sing. At that moment, I realised that pleasure comes from inside. I'd had showers before, but they'd never felt so wonderful. I realised that if my mind was clear, even the simplest things could be ecstatic. (And I didn't need to be fabulously rich in order to buy happiness.)

So nowadays, I similarly focus on the pure sensations of having a shower: the smell of soap, the sounds and texture of water, the warmth and skin response, the pleasurable bodily movements. Of course, I don't meditate on showering every time I shower, but it is an option I take up two or three times a week. I always notice how lovely it feels and consciously appreciate it. It confirms the basic formula: if you want to be relaxed, be more sensual.

Showering naturally leads into another meditation: getting dressed (and getting ready to go out). If you think I'm inventing this as an easy option for busy Westerners, you've got it wrong.

I'll let you in on a secret. The Buddha, in fact, was a bit of a fuss-pot, and he insisted that his monks always look neat and tidy when they went out. If they were sloppy in their dress and behaviour, he said, it would reflect badly on him and his reputation. He was rather like a boarding-school headmaster who wanted his boys to have their shirt-tails tucked in and their hair combed when they went to town.

The Buddha was an inveterate rule-maker and inventor of meditation practices, so he asked his monks to meditate on getting dressed. After monks are sitting for a while, their robes, which are just pieces of cloth wrapped around their bodies, get somewhat slack. When they stand up, they are required to spend quite some time making sure their robes hang properly and look nice. You'll notice Buddhist monks being slow and deliberate about this even now, in the twenty-first century. It's in their rules of monkly etiquette.

If your partner, therefore, is annoyed about the time you take in front of your make-up mirror, just tell them you're practising an ancient Buddhist meditation. If he goes off in a huff, you can accuse him of religious insensitivity!

IRONING

The easiest kinds of household tasks to turn into meditations are those that are relatively short, repetitive and have clear boundaries. Ten minutes of ironing, for example, is ideal. This naturally divides into three or four separate tasks: setting up the ironing board and the iron; doing the ironing itself; putting away the clothes, and then the ironing board when you've finished.

Ironing is not intellectually demanding, but it does require a certain amount of attention to do it well. The movements are simple, but they need to be smooth and rhythmic. The more attention you give to it, the more satisfying the results. In other words, you can check how relaxed and focused you are by the way the clothes look afterwards!

When you iron, don't forget your faithful ally, the breath. Although you mostly focus on the actual activity, still keep a background awareness of your posture and your breathing. They will tell you immediately whether you are relaxing or simply holding on.

WASHING DISHES

Like ironing, washing the dishes is simple and repetitive, and yet it still needs some attention to be done well. You can see how people who are house-proud can get a certain quiet satisfaction out of cleaning up the kitchen properly. We can all do the dishes, but to do them well and enjoy it is another matter.

Washing up is a more spectacular activity than ironing. There's more splash, noise and texture, and the movements are more varied and faster. We often try to rush through it, but washing up can still be done smoothly and elegantly.

I suggest you try to notice the very end of each little action, and actually *finish* it before you start the next. Often we will virtually throw a cup into the rack with our mind already leaping on to the next action. I suggest you deliberately place the cup down – it won't take you any longer – and rest there for a fraction of a second before you do the next thing.

TIDYING UP

After an hour or two of computer work or study, I like to take a break. I could have a drink or go for a walk, but once or twice a day I simply potter around for five or ten minutes, tidying up. There are always bits of paper or clothing where they shouldn't be, a few unwashed dishes or food that needs to be put away. I like the way something will catch my eye and lead me from one room to the next, where something else will take me on another tangent.

If I resolved to spend an hour putting the whole house in order, it would feel like a chore. Five or ten minutes of tidying up, however, are a pleasant distraction from the sedentary nature of head work. I enjoy the fact that my body is moving and breathing more easily – it's a relief to get out of the chair. I like the bending, touching, lifting and placing. I enjoy the glimpses of the garden beyond the windows.

OTHER POSSIBLE ACTIVITIES

What activities at home do you find relaxing? You can get more pleasure out of many of them by meditating on them. Simple, repetitive things with a lot of natural sensory input are best. Watering the garden or walking the dog is better than watching TV or reading a book, for example.

There are lots of possibilities, nonetheless: washing the car; weeding or planting; simple DIY tasks; carrying out the rubbish; hanging out the washing; making the bed. The simplicity is the key. It is as if you leave behind the intellectual demands of your life in the twenty-first century and revert to the simple life of a Victorian servant.

This is easy to understand but more difficult to apply. Earlier on (*see page 109*) I asked you to focus on just one thing – such as the breath or sounds. In these household meditations, however, the mind is naturally shifting through many of the senses. It may not stay with any one for more than a few seconds.

You remain in the present whether you focus on one sensation or many. However, if the mind moves too quickly, it may fail to settle. It's also more prone to succumb to the temptation of thinking, and to forget what it's trying to do. So it takes a little effort to get the best out of these practices. Here are some suggestions that might help.

It's good to have a slogan in the mind: 'be sensual', or 'be present'. You could actually 'name' the activity each time you breathe out: 'ironing', 'washing' or whatever. You could periodically ask yourself, 'Where am I?' and notice what is actually in your mind at that moment.

It's even more useful to be systematic. None of these meditations will amount to much unless you repeat it. I suggest you do a meditation at least four times over four days to get the hang of it.

So choose your meditation and stick to it. The best ones are those that are relatively short and have clear start and finish points. The two minutes it takes to make a cup of tea, for example, is ideal. Actually drinking the tea would not be so easy. It's hard to stay focused for ten minutes or so. Below is a summary of this technique.

Household Meditations

Spend a few seconds relaxing your body and breathing.

Start any activity that has a clear start and finish.

Be sensual. Be present. Enjoy the sensations.

If it helps, 'name' the activity as you breathe out.

Occasionally check: 'Where am I?'

Go for sensory detail. Get into the rhythm of the activity.

Check your body and your breath periodically to make sure you are relaxing.

If you find you are distracted, sigh and return.

24. Going to the toilet

IT'S QUITE RELAXING to go to the toilet. At least one sphincter has to relax completely or it's not worth going there at all. When you let one muscle go, others can relax in sympathy. Furthermore, the toilet may be the only place where no one will disturb you. You can always grab a few extra seconds there and no one will complain.

The Buddha was the first person to recommend urinating as a meditation object. This is a practice that is at least 2,500 years old. A psychologist friend reminded me of this recently. He says he goes to the toilet in the five minutes between clients, and lets *everything* go along with the urine. He gets so relaxed in those few seconds he says he can barely hold his balance.

In Western literature, it is surprising how often the toilet is regarded as a suitable place for deep thought. You sit down and settle into your body. You relax and wait, and randomly survey the state of the nation. Not surprisingly, bright ideas can arise and you feel relaxed for minutes afterwards. An excellent meditation!

Going to the Toilet

As you approach the toilet, **sigh** *in anticipation.*

Get out of your head and into your body.
Feel the pressure in your bladder.

As you urinate, close your eyes and **sigh** *deeply.*

Feel all the muscles of your body loosening in sympathy.

Don't hurry to finish. No one will disturb you.

After the last drop, stay motionless for a few seconds more.
Enjoy that space, with nothing to do.

Walk away with a smile on your face.

25. In the car

IN MY EARLY YEARS as a teacher, I was afraid that students who meditated while driving would relax too much and have a crash. So I told them firmly: 'Don't meditate while driving! A few seconds asleep at the wheel is enough to kill you.' I would add the fact that an estimated 15 per cent of fatal accidents are caused by drivers who fall asleep.

Yet despite my voice-of-doom admonishments, I found my students would still meditate while driving. In fact, rather than killing themselves they usually reported that they were driving more safely, getting fewer speeding tickets and being more tolerant towards the idiots on the road. By meditating, they seemed more likely to avoid accidents rather than cause them. Since they were doing it anyway, I decided to teach them how to do it safely. But first, let me describe how to meditate while the car is stationary.

MEDITATING AT THE RED LIGHTS

I took many radio interviews when the original edition of this book came out in 1993. The interviewers were fascinated by the idea that you could meditate in the forty-five seconds you were stuck at a red light. In fact, a television team invited me to fly across Australia to Melbourne so I could demonstrate this.

A team of eight people with a back-up truck met me at the airport. The car had a camera mounted on the bonnet, pointing to the driver's seat. It was a grey winter's day, so the technicians had put bright lights within the car itself, shining up on my face. I drove off into rush-hour traffic, late on a dismal Friday afternoon, to demonstrate the Red Light Meditation. It wasn't easy.

This exercise works best if you are running late and the traffic lights turn red as you approach.

Red Light Meditation

You have been given a whole minute to stop and do nothing.
Relax. Shake yourself loose and settle back into the seat.

Take three or four ***deep breaths*** *and* ***sigh****.*

Scan your body for tension.
How are you holding the steering wheel?
Are your face and neck muscles tighter than necessary?

Let your belly soften. Keep breathing.

Be present. Look around you slowly.
Notice the scenery, the traffic, the sky.

The exercise finishes when the lights turn green.
Now devote all your attention to the task at hand:
drive safely, and look forward to the next red light.

WHEN THE CAR IS PARKED

I often run seminars or workshops in the city. I cannot take parking for granted, so I allow myself an extra five minutes or so to find a space. As a result, I'm usually in the parking building a few minutes before I need to get out of the car.

Often my mind is restless with anticipation, so I deliberately meditate to slow it down. I hear the engine die away as I switch off the ignition. I put my head against the headrest, and wait for the vibrations of the road to leave my body. I scan my body over seven deep breaths (by doing the Countdown exercise, *see page 40*), or scan more slowly, three or four breaths in each region, if I've got the time. Within that short space, I try to go as close to the sleep zone as possible.

It's good to have events or places as starting cues for a meditation. Nearly every time I'm in a parking building, I'll meditate before I get out and start moving. It's a wonderful point of hiatus. It's where I briefly stop the world and get off, and no one notices. One of my best students told me she regularly leaves home early when she drives somewhere, so she will have time to meditate in the car at the other end.

Another cue place for me is the parking lot at the supermarket. I don't meditate in the car since there's no reason to wait, but I deliberately stay in the present when I get out. I consciously reach for the door handle, feeling the texture and resistance as I open it. I notice the surprisingly complex body movements that go with getting up from the seat.

... meditating at the red light

As I usually do when I stand up, I take three or four deep breaths to get myself into a good walking posture. Then I walk, taking in the sight of the trees and the sky, and feeling the air on my body. A minute later, I'm in the supermarket. The meditation is now over, but it was a minute well spent.

NOTICE WHEN YOU'RE NOT DRIVING SAFELY

It's quite possible to drive across town while lost in reverie, not noticing or remembering a single detail of the journey. Most people can even get home if they're drunk or stoned, or in the first stages of age-related dementia. To be honest, driving doesn't require a lot of our attention, so many people do use it as an opportunity to space out and generally escape the pressures of the day.

That is the scary truth of driving: people are often absent when they drive. Another truth is that driver inattention, not even involving the driver falling asleep, is the cause of 30 per cent of fatal accidents. In other words, the vast majority of times you will get home safely, but once or twice in a decade you may be in a serious accident.

The ideal state for driving involves you being both relaxed and alert. You become a menace on the roads if you're either too wired up or too sleepy. If you're stressed out, you'll be too preoccupied with your thoughts to notice the road, and your responses are likely to be impulsive and thoughtless. For safe driving, it's important to get out of the high-stress zone.

Unfortunately, when you do relax somewhat, the body may want to keep relaxing. If you're exhausted after a long, hard day, you can drop rapidly from a suitably alert state into drowsiness. That's when you notice a momentary mental blankness, or the eyes want to close, or the head bobs. Those are clear signs that you need to wake up if you want to stay alive. If you cannot pull over and have a few minutes rest, at least open the window, breathe more deeply and consciously look around you.

HOW TO MEDITATE SAFELY WHILE DRIVING

First let me suggest that you only try a driving meditation after you've already learned to meditate in a safer environment. When people learn to meditate, they are often astonished at how quickly they can relax. Although they can be very stressed and wired up when they start, a minute later they're at the point of sleep. Until you realise this, it's not safe to meditate while driving.

Second, when driving don't focus exclusively on the breath or the body. Focus instead on the activity of driving. This means tuning into a variety of different sensations in succession. Notice the world around you: the traffic, the sky, the scenery. Also notice your breathing and muscle tension, but don't let your mind settle there as you would in a normal sitting meditation.

There is a general rule in meditation: focusing on one thing such as the breath takes you deep – eventually putting you into a trance state – because it eliminates other sensory input. While this is wonderful to do when you're sitting safely in a room, it's dangerous when you are driving. It can take you from a state of alertness to the borders of sleep in a flash.

This is why it's not good to focus on any one thing for long. Scan instead, by focusing on many things in succession. Don't focus on the breath or the body exclusively. Focus on the activity of driving. Be mindful: go for a wide-angle awareness rather than pinpoint focus. Don't leave the outside world behind. Be present. And wake yourself up quickly when you realise you're falling asleep.

Driving Meditation

Notice where you are: what is happening around you?

Without taking your attention off the road,
check your breathing. Is it loose and comfortable?

Check your posture. Are you unnecessarily tense?

Let your mind oscillate between inner and outer.

Enjoy what you see: the sky, scenery, people and cars, but don't dwell with any one thing more than two to three seconds.
Let your mind scan continuously.

Ask yourself periodically: 'Am I in the present?'

Be vigilant for the first signs of drowsiness.
If you get sleepy, take immediate action to wake yourself up.

26. When you have to wait

YEARS AGO, I WORKED IN KYOTO in Japan, and on Wednesday nights I had to catch five separate trains to get home from Osaka. I would get off one train and walk to another platform to find my next one waiting. The subway schedule was so exquisitely synchronised that I only had to wait on platforms or in stationary trains for eleven minutes in total. I didn't waste a single minute staring in frustration into dark tunnels.

Nowadays we're always waiting. For buses or trains, in traffic jams, at red lights, for children outside schools and in supermarket or bank queues. We wait for the TV ads to pass, for the boring lecture or meeting to be over, for the meal to cook. We wait to fall asleep and, if we wake early, we wait until it's time to get up. We wait for someone to go or someone to come.

We're all so busy and yet we waste so much time unable to do anything. If we could have all those wasted minutes in one big, juicy hunk of maybe an hour each day, we could do something with them. Instead they dribble away, a minute here and a minute there, and it's a terrible waste.

Waiting usually makes us frustrated and irritable. We grind our teeth and fume, and our blood pressure and metabolic rate shoot up. We use the opportunity to get even more tense than we are already. We can burn a huge amount of energy while doing nothing at all. Usually, you cannot even think productively while waiting for a queue to move.

It doesn't need to be this way. Waiting gives us a perfect opportunity to destress. It could be the best chance you get all day to go inwards and relax. You don't need much time at all. In fact, the more stressed you are, the more benefit you get from a spot meditation. A few deep breaths and a change of attitude will take you out of the stress zone within seconds.

BORING MEETINGS

While we wait, we usually have to be semi-alert. It's considered to be bad form to put your head on the table and go to sleep at a meeting or lecture, or in a waiting room, even though doing so could be best for everyone concerned. Because your eyes have to be open, it's most natural to do a visual object meditation in these circumstances.

To do this you settle your eyes on something and let them soften. You can focus on the grain of the boardroom table, the hair of the person in front of you, the pattern on a chair or dress, or the angles of furniture. Don't stare at your object blankly, but gently explore it, as if it were fascinating and important. Usually the object is neither, but the state of mind that you are entering *is* important. If you can relax frequently during the day, you are more likely to be healthy and productive than if you run on high anxiety.

PUBLIC TRANSPORT

If you often travel by train, bus, taxi or plane, you have a god-given opportunity to do a *long* meditation regularly. A few years ago I flew from Perth in Western Australia to San Francisco in the United States. When I realised I would have thirty-two hours between bed and bed, I decided to meditate for as much of the journey as I could to make it less of an ordeal.

Since meditation is a state of 'non-doing', I literally did as little as possible. I didn't read books or newspapers, watch the in-flight movies, talk to people or listen to the scratchy music on the headphones. While sitting, I simply scanned my body continuously and monitored my thoughts and moods, for hours at a time.

Whenever I had to move, I did so slowly and deliberately.

There was no need to hurry. It wouldn't get me there any faster. I even spoke more slowly at check-in counters, and ate my food and went to the toilet more deliberately.

Because I was sitting so much, I particularly relished the times I had to walk through airport corridors, down the plane aisle or through the street. Whenever I had to stand, I used the opportunity to open up my posture and breathe as deeply and smoothly as possible.

The trip was still exhausting. I remember slipping into dream states while going through customs in Honolulu, Hawaii. Yet it was also very lovely. I had thirty-two hours to do nothing at all – what a relief! I've never had that since.

Some people instinctively learn the art of waiting. Last year I spend a couple of weeks training workers on the oil rigs off the coast of Western Australia, and I saw the demands of that kind of life. Each fortnight, they catch the early morning two-hour flight from Perth to Karratha, and then the one-hour flight by helicopter across the ocean to the rig. Many of them, in fact, travelled far more than this.

When flying with the oil workers, I realised that most of them already knew about conserving their energy. They mostly sat there immobile with their eyes closed, almost asleep the whole time. While on the rig, I also discovered that people didn't rush around. Because the culture of safety was paramount (and the risks so huge), no one moved fast or did anything impulsively. Despite the forty degrees of heat and the twelve-hour shifts, it was a surprisingly relaxing way to work. Some of these men had mastered the arts of waiting and moving deliberately. Their jobs demanded it.

MEDITATING WHILE STANDING

Waiting is not so much a new meditation as a new posture and situation in which to meditate. People generally sit or walk to meditate, but waiting often requires you to stand. Let me explain how to go about it.

Let's assume you are in a supermarket queue and you'll obviously have to wait two or three minutes. Rather than getting frustrated, you can say to yourself: 'Wonderful! I've now got a chance to slow down and relax. I'll be able to drop some of the tension I've been carrying all day.'

So how do you meditate while standing? First, you may discover that it is impossible to stand still. We really need a third leg to be perfectly immobile. We all naturally sway and shuffle around when we stand, and you can use that movement to loosen up the body. Just remember that standing is a naturally mobile position, even if you seem to be going nowhere.

While in a queue, you have to keep your eyes open, of course. If your eyes are restless, your mind will be also, so settle them gently on something in front of you. The shoulder of the next person will do just fine. When you've anchored your gaze, let the eyes soften so they're almost out of focus.

Now check your posture and breathing. If you're holding yourself rigid, it's quite easy to loosen up almost immediately. Take three or four deep breaths and bring your body into balance.

If you still have another minute or so, do the Countdown Meditation (*see page 40*), where you scan the body over seven breaths. Alternatively, you could simply breathe deeply and evenly, making the breath more rhythmic and loose as long as possible. Or you could focus on something visual and gently examine it, as if was important.

There tend to be many distractions when you wait, so it's useful to silently talk to yourself. If you're looking at a blue object, say the word 'blue' as you breathe. If you're scanning your body, count the breaths from seven to one as you do so. If you're simply focused on the breath, say 'in, out' as you breathe. Or you could say an affirmation. Childish as these devices seem, they all remind you what you are doing and keep you on track. Even if your mind wanders, the words often continue of their own momentum and call you back.

Standing Meditation

Loosen up your body as you wait. Stand comfortably.

Take a ***few deep breaths*** *and* ***sigh****.*

Settle your eyes on something, and let your gaze soften.

Now do whatever meditation appeals to you:
Deep Breathing,
Or *Countdown.*
Or *Visual Object Meditation.*

It is useful to count the breaths, or 'name' the object, or to say an affirmation as you breathe, to keep you occupied.

Expect to be distracted, but don't drop the meditation.

Feel your body relaxing.

27. How to fall asleep

BY SWITCHING ON the body's relaxation response, meditation takes you down towards sleep. In fact, if you're lying down after a few hours of activity, it's quite hard to stay awake at all. It still amazes me how deeply people can relax while holding themselves upright on a chair or a cushion. They may even say afterwards, 'My body vanished. I felt I was completely gone. It was a beautiful state.' Yet they still stay sufficiently awake to stop themselves from falling over.

After eight years of teaching maybe 10,000 students in all, I was asked in class, 'Has anyone ever fallen off the chair?' I was able to categorically answer, 'I've never seen it happen once.' God obviously heard me, so in the very next class, with a different group of people, a man fell off his chair.

He may have been on some kind of medication. He fell into the lap of the woman next to him and remained sleeping. I quickly went behind him and raised him up in his chair. I held him in position for a few minutes while continuing to lead the meditation, and eventually let him go. At the end of the session, he asked, 'Did I fall asleep?' That was the first and last time anyone has ever fallen off a chair in my classes.

THE TWO-MINUTE NAP

So, even in a public place, you can afford to relax deeply with the confidence that you won't snooze off and start drooling. In those circumstances, you never fall asleep totally. Your guardian angel is looking out for you, so don't feel shy about relaxing as deeply as you need to.

If you're exhausted, you need to go to sleep. It's as simple as that, and it doesn't matter if it's 10 a.m. or 3.15 p.m. See if you can grab a minute or two to sleep while staying upright. Just a minute at the edge of sleep will switch off your compulsive thinking and let you start anew. Australian sleep researchers found, to their surprise, that you don't actually have to fall asleep to work off some of your 'sleep debt'. You can benefit hugely from just briefly touching the edge of sleep.

If you are really tired during the day you hardly need a technique to help you relax. You just give yourself permission to mentally collapse, while staying in an upright position to keep control. It often helps if you say the words, 'sleep', or 'let go', as you breathe.

Go and sit in the toilet for a couple of minutes. Close your eyes when on public transport and disappear. When I was at school, I used to sit in my car at lunchtime. I was meditating even when I was fifteen! You'll be amazed at how quickly you can fall asleep, if you give yourself half a chance.

Of course, it would be much nicer to lie down for an hour and crash out completely, but can you afford to do that? The art of spot meditating, let me remind you, involves finding the neglected spaces in the day and using them. You don't need to reschedule your life in order to relax.

WHY FALLING ASLEEP CAN BE SO DIFFICULT

Insomnia, in all its pathological forms, is a huge problem in our speedy and over-bright world. It is both a cause and an effect of stress, depression, exhaustion and many lifestyle illnesses. I suspect most of our misery and sickness would vanish if we could simply sleep as well as people did a hundred years ago. (They averaged two hours a night more than we do now.)

Going to bed seems like the obvious time to relax and fall asleep, but this can be more difficult than it seems. If being in bed is the first time you've stopped 'doing' things all day long, the mind can say, 'Great! Now I've got time to think about all that stuff.' So you can be horribly exhausted and yet your chattering mind won't let you fall asleep.

Conversely, you may be so worn out that you fall asleep, but a few hours later you're wide awake. You've rested just enough for your overly stimulated mind to get going again. It's a pity that it's only 2 a.m. The mind has things to do.

Generally, if you meditate while lying down, you fall asleep within a minute or two. Most of us carry enough latent fatigue to tip us into sleep, given half the chance. The body has a natural inclination towards balance, and if you're tired, it naturally draws you down towards sleep. Meditation works because it helps you bypass the chronic mental activity that keeps you awake.

If you lie in bed and think, however, you're quite likely to still be awake fifteen or thirty minutes later. It now becomes even harder to fall asleep, because your body has actually rested somewhat and is not as tired as it was a few minutes earlier. You've failed to capitalise on that natural wave of fatigue that occurs as soon as you lie down. Similarly, it can be hard to go back to sleep at 3 a.m precisely because the body *has* partly rested. It doesn't need sleep as much as it did at 10 p.m.

TO FALL ASLEEP, FOCUS INTENTLY

Many people can only find time to meditate when they're in bed, trying to fall asleep. In fact, it's a perfect opportunity. I invariably meditate to go to sleep, or put myself back to sleep when I wake at night. It rarely takes more than a minute or two.

When in bed, our thoughts tend to be vague and rambling, yet even though they're going around in circles, they can still keep us awake. Paradoxically, the way to fall asleep is to focus intently, in fact making the mind as sharp as possible. This is the only way to escape the rambling thoughts. You cannot waffle your way into sleep.

Forget about counting sheep. Counting the breaths is much better, but don't be lazy about it. Don't lose the count. Check that you actually feel the end and start of each breath. This is the kind of precise focus you need to escape the thoughts that are keeping you awake. Deep focus automatically relaxes you. It is the royal road into the trance states. If you're at all sleepy and your mind becomes very focused, it is almost impossible to stay awake while lying in bed.

... forget about counting sheep

Another option while in bed includes listening to the sounds around you. You can switch on a piece of music – I have my stereo remote on my bedside table; if I wake in the night I can switch on music without even turning on the light.

Even if meditation fails to put you back to sleep, the benefits can be huge. If you lie awake and think all night, you burn a lot of energy and get up in the morning frustrated and exhausted.

If, on the other hand, you meditate through the small hours, you will rest and conserve energy even though you will still be awake. You'll also be more likely to dip in and out of sleep for a few minutes here and there.

While not perfect, this is vastly preferable to fretting all night. One of my students was in such pain that he rarely slept for more than half an hour at a time. Then he took up meditating. He found that although he still remained awake for much of the night, meditating in the small hours allowed him to rest far more deeply than he had for years. This gave him much more energy to run his two businesses during the day. He was very happy with the results of his night-time meditations.

The spot meditation below is a kind of 'virtual' sleep, to give you a quick shot of restful time during the working day.

Two-Minute Nap

Whenever you're exhausted, let yourself fall asleep.
All you need is a place where you can sit and close your eyes.

Say the words, 'Let go,' or 'Sleep,' as you breathe.

Soften the muscles. Let your body feel heavy and soft.

Go to the very edge, but don't fall off the chair.

Enjoy the oblivion and inactivity.

When you have to, get up and get going again.

Falling Asleep

Lie on your back – this is usually best.

Choose your meditation: Breathing Deeply, Body Scan or Sounds.

Focus as intently as you can, even if you constantly lose focus.

Go for detail. Even a minute's worth can put you to sleep.

If you remain awake, tell yourself, 'At least I'm relaxing.'

PART FOUR

FINAL THOUGHTS

28. Am I doing it right?

FROM THE OUTSIDE, the meditations in this book don't look like 'real' meditations at all. They demand no special behaviour, location or even time, and certainly no allegiance to a spiritual tradition. Since you do them in the course of ordinary activities they're virtually invisible. So what makes an eating meditation different from, well, just eating?

It's about where your mind is. If you eat while thinking of other things, that's just eating and you won't relax much. If, on the other hand, you consciously focus on the sensations of eating, you'll relax rapidly and your mind will become calm and clear. That's a meditation.

Appearances can deceive. A person in a Buddhist centre, sitting cross-legged with his eyes closed for an hour, may be completely unfocused and not meditating at all. He could be daydreaming, falling asleep or thinking about everything at random. Conversely, someone who is fully present while preparing food or walking to the shops is meditating beautifully.

It's true that some meditators really are spaced-out, gloomy navel gazers who have turned their backs on the world. It does amaze me that a technique designed to minimise thought and bring you into the present can be used for completely the opposite purpose.

It all comes back to how you focus, but focusing requires some attention. Our minds are very mercurial and can scatter over the entire universe within seconds. Amid all the temptations, we cannot expect them to stay peacefully in one place unsupervised. You need to continually monitor what the mind is actually doing if you want quality in your meditation. In particular, you need to know when you are focused, and when you are not.

One way to sharpen your practice is to ask questions as you meditate:

- ***'Am I focused?'***
- ***'Am I in the present?'***
- ***'What is happening right now?'***
- ***'Am I relaxing or not?'***

This makes you more self-aware and observant and usually improves your state of mind immediately.

AM I FOCUSED? AM I WELL FOCUSED?

Whenever you meditate, you need to consciously focus on something – the breath, the body, sounds, an activity or whatever. This sounds obvious, but I mention it because some people simply 'try to relax' without focusing at all. This is like trying to drive a car without a steering wheel.

So choose your object and during the meditation periodically ask yourself, 'Am I focused?' You'll often find you're not as focused as you thought you were, but at least you know what to do: come back to focus. That's what actually works.

Then it's good to go for *quality* focus. Sometimes, you're focused but not very well. You could be tracking the breaths but still indulging some train of thought in the background. If you focus better, the results can be dramatic. You'll find time seems to slow down and you notice more detail. You'll catch the exact moment the breath stops, for example, or notice a colour or flavour with heightened sensitivity. It's when you can say to yourself, 'Yes. I'm really there, and I know it.'

Deepening your focus is what takes you from an 'okay' meditation into excellence. If you let go of the background conversations, you can slip from moderate relaxation into a delicious stillness and clarity of mind. It's the difference between just being relaxed and truly meditating.

AM I IN THE PRESENT?

It's very common to shift your point of focus in a meditation. You might start with the breath, but you may soon find you're more aware of a pain in your body, the sound of birds or traffic, or even a smell or taste.

The initial object of focus is like your doorway into the world of the senses. Once you're there, you don't need to stand at the threshold. If you focus on anything sensual, it will distance you from thought. In fact, scanning the sensory environment will often keep you more present than trying to hold on to one thing to the exclusion of others.

Of course, thoughts also occur in the present moment, and sometimes they need to be acknowledged. If something is troubling you, just ask, 'What is this?' and identify it. It's extremely useful to notice what you're thinking and feeling, even if it's unpleasant.

AM I RELAXING?

It's good to be inventive when you meditate, but people are often unsure if what they're doing is right. Some focus on two or three things at once, such as the breath and sounds. Others may explore a headache or stomach pain. Some focus on colours or dream images that mysteriously appear as they relax. Some say, 'I only meditate while walking the dog,' or 'I only do it on the bus to work, or while swimming in the pool.'

The truth is that there are thousands of different ways to relax and calm the mind. It's not what you do that matters, but whether it actually works. Meditation can be defined as any technique that relaxes the body quickly and calms the mind, yet people often forget this. So when a student says to me, 'Is it okay if I do this or that?' I ask him, 'Well, did it work? Do you feel more relaxed and mentally clear as a result?'

If you check your body, you'll soon know when you're tense, when you're relaxing and when you're fully relaxed. Similarly, you should know when your mind is slowing down and becoming calmer and clearer. There doesn't need to be any mystery about this.

The most obvious physical signs of relaxation are:

- *The body feeling heavy or still or numb.*
- *A mild tingling or warmth on the skin.*
- *A heightened awareness of little aches and pains, and latent fatigue.*
- *The breath becoming soft and loose.*

There are other signs as well, but most people will pick up at least two or three of the above.

Similarly, the mental signs of relaxation are:

- *A slower mind.*
- *A passive awareness of peripheral thoughts and sensations.*
- *An emotional detachment – neither liking nor disliking what is happening.*
- *A sense of stillness and peace.*

If you are getting some of the above effects, then whatever you're doing in your meditation is obviously working.

AM I MORE RELAXED THAN I WAS?

Many people are dissatisfied with short (and long) meditations because they still don't make them totally relaxed. They feel they have to attain an ideal state of mental blankness or bliss for meditation to be worthwhile at all. They say things like, 'I tried to meditate but I couldn't get there.'

Aiming for an ideal state, particularly one that you've never achieved before, is bound to lead to disappointment. It's more sensible to regard meditation as a skill that you develop in thousands of small incremental steps. You cannot expect to play a Beethoven sonata perfectly the first time you sit at the piano.

So look for improvement, not perfection. After any meditation, ask, 'Am I more relaxed than I was before?' You'll invariably find that you are, and that makes it worth doing. Nearly any meditation will relax the body and calm the mind to some degree.

Relaxation doesn't always equate to physical comfort. Nor does mental clarity mean you are totally happy. If you're sick, in pain or going through a relationship break-up, it won't all vanish when you meditate. You can still be physically relaxed and relatively clear-minded about it, but don't expect to feel perfectly happy as well. If you're seriously stressed, it will take more than one meditation to feel good again.

CHECK WHAT YOU'RE DOING

Meditation is often presented as a hypnotic technique that blanks out thoughts, giving you a kind of mental stupefaction if you do it correctly. Just occasionally, this can happen, particularly if you are in a religious or group setting that provides a strong, supportive atmosphere. Because this mindless state is both rare and idealised, people often get dependent on teachers and groups, seeking it out. In fact, I don't think it is either useful or healthy.

To become good at anything requires some active intelligence. Although meditating marginalises thought, you still need to evaluate what you are doing and understand the process. This is why talking to teachers and other meditators is so useful. Even on your own, in the middle of a meditation, you can examine what you are doing by asking questions such as these:

- *'Am I focused?'*
- *'If not, what am I thinking about?'*
- *'Can I focus better?'*
- *'Am I in the present?'*
- *'Am I relaxing?'*
- *'What is going on, right now?'*
- *'How does my body feel?'*
- *'What mood am I in?'*

29. What else can I do?

SPOT MEDITATIONS CANNOT CURE EVERYTHING. If you work in a city and relate to other people, you're bound to be exposed to stressors whose effects you cannot totally neutralise with meditation. If you also overwork, or are sick or in personal strife for too long, then misery and ill-health are almost guaranteed. You'll need more than a few spot meditations to manage your stress.

Let me give you some suggestions. First of all, it's essential to get an accurate diagnosis: know what your stressors are and how much you respond to them. I meet many people who say, 'Yes, work is stressful, but I'm handling it fairly well.' In fact, they're fooling themselves. If you could ask their bodies, they would say, 'Work is killing me!' We usually know the main causes of our stress but rarely notice the minor ones, and we invariably underestimate their total, long-term effect on us.

It's crucial to know exactly *what* stresses you and *how much* you respond to it. The exercises in this book help you to become sensitive to your physiological stress markers, so you can destress to some degree immediately. Meditation will ameliorate the bad effects considerably, but at a certain point you may have to ask, 'Can I afford to go on like this?' If you're suffering from continual insomnia, indigestion, and neck and shoulder pain, and your breathing is rigid, you may need to look at something more than spot meditating.

If you are prepared to devote the time, you have many options. You can:

- *Meditate longer and better.*
- *Look at getting better exercise, diet and sleep.*

- ***Identify what stresses you and avoid it as much as you can.***
- ***Actively pursue what relaxes you and makes you feel good.***

LONGER AND BETTER MEDITATION

People often tell me, 'I enjoy the spot meditations so much that they keep getting longer. I found myself meditating for twenty-five minutes yesterday.' The first two or three minutes are the most time-efficient part of any meditation, but the longer and more often you meditate, the more the body and mind can repair themselves.

Getting better quality is not so easy. There are problems in longer meditations that don't occur as much in short ones. For example, you often relax so deeply that you more or less fall asleep. Pleasant as this is, it's not much different from normal sleep. Your mind will still be active below the surface of consciousness, and you'll emerge with a foggy rather than a clear mind.

Even if you don't fall asleep, your mind is much more inclined to wander in a long meditation. Like sleep, this can be a pleasant state, but you're not getting the best possible results. You won't get much clarity of mind if you doze and ramble.

It's easy to stretch short meditations into long ones, but to get quality it's best to learn more about the complexities of this skill by attending classes or retreats. If you like the approach to meditation in this book, I suggest you seek out Buddhist groups rather than Hindu ones. The practices here come mostly from the Buddhist 'mindfulness' or 'awareness' tradition, with a secondary input from the yoga tradition.

You could also read more books and, once again, I suggest those with a Buddhist orientation. The most comprehensive introduction is Jack Kornfield's book *A Path with Heart*.

Piatkus Books also publish my two other books: *Teach Yourself to Meditate* and *How Meditation Heals*. You can also look up my website for extra resources such as CDs and correspondence courses: perthmeditationcentre.com.au.

EXERCISE, DIET AND SLEEP

As a teacher, I naturally meditate a lot, but if I didn't also exercise, eat and sleep well, I know I would be miserable. A golfing friend said recently that he feels so wonderful when he walks out of a yoga class that he's committing himself to it seriously this year and giving up on his therapy groups. 'Therapy never made me feel this good,' he said.

I'm sure I don't need to tell you that good exercise, diet and sleep are important for your well-being. Let me suggest, however, that they are more important than you think they are. If you possibly can, pay more attention to them. You may be wealthy and successful and have a full social schedule, but unless you do basic body maintenance your quality of life is bound to be mediocre. And if you do more than just the basics, you're almost guaranteed to be much happier.

KNOW WHAT STRESSES YOU AND AVOID IT

Stress is not always negative. It's just a state of arousal, and anything exciting or stimulating will stir up the body. We all seek it out: it's a key ingredient for success in any field. In fact, life would be very flat and depressing if we were never aroused at all.

It's obvious that you should avoid stressors you don't like, but what do you do with those that you love? The workaholic, the obsessive sportsperson, the socialiser, the busy working mother could all be enjoying their lives enormously. They just wish they had more time in the day, not to rest but to do more things! Most of us are at least mildly addicted to what stimulates and gratifies us, even if it's just TV or the Internet.

It seems so unfair that enjoyable things can also be bad for our health. Late-night TV, stimulating work and social activities will keep your body and mind awake long past their bedtime and there's a price to pay for that. Coffee and thrills cannot wipe out the damage of yet another bad night's sleep. A satisfying life can still give you panic attacks, migraines and a stroke at fifty.

You don't have to withdraw to a hermitage to avoid stress, but you might have to make some lifestyle choices, particularly as you get older. You can save your muscles and joints by shifting from a high stress sport to a low stress one. Don't stay out with your mates so late: save your brain. You can save your digestive system by eating and drinking more moderately. Plan for a longer wind-down time after work or sex or exercise.

It's natural for younger people to seek excellence through a single-minded obsession. 'I need to know how good I could be,' says the woman who sacrifices everything else for her sport or career. If you want high arousal and motivation and many wonderful pleasures, it's natural to push that stress button as often and as hard as you can.

Exciting as this is, in my view this is an adolescent way of operating that doesn't work well as you get older. I think that ageing is about becoming more self-aware and intelligent, and seeking a balanced life rather than excellence. It is about compromise: being good at the many things necessary for a good life rather than being brilliant at any one of them.

In fact, becoming a mature human being is surprisingly difficult. Finding balance is the big challenge of the middle years, and it does take a considerable degree of intelligence. It's not just a matter of fiddling with the details – we all do that anyway. Understanding your own character and capacities intimately, and undoing the illusions and habits of the past, is usually an inner journey that takes years.

Finding a healthy balance means understanding your body and its changing needs for stimulation and rest. When you're younger, you can play hard and collapse afterwards, and you survive. A few days of self-abuse don't kill you. When you're older you have to manage stress with more sensitivity. For example, a sedentary life and bad sleep are bound to make you miserable to some degree, and you cannot avoid that fact forever.

SEEK OUT WHAT RELAXES YOU

Obviously, meditation is not the only way to relax. Many pleasures stimulate us, but others have a soothing effect and they're worth seeking out. The best are slow and sensual: stroking a cat, walking in the park or eating, listening to music, gardening or craft work, dancing or slow yoga, writing a letter (not an email!) or a journal. If you're feeling tired and stressed, there could be nothing better than a long cuddle on the couch with your lover.

Most of the above activities are solitary ones. There is invariably a low-level tension and excitement that comes from being in the company of others. To relax at all, we need at least a little time to ourselves, even if we do nothing with it. I am sure this is why so many people now choose to live alone. When they enter their homes, they are finally the masters of their own space and time. When alone, you unconsciously revert to your own natural rhythms of movement and rest, which may be quite unlike the rhythms of the city and the people around you.

Most of us need more 'down-time', though it is difficult to know what to do with it when we get it. It is useful to remember that meditation is actually the art of doing nothing.

... seek out what relaxes you

It is extremely nourishing to 'just be'. That's when your body repairs itself and your mind files away the input of the preceding hours and days. The less you do, the better they can perform their inner work. So don't feel bad about being unproductive in your spare time. It's more valuable than you can possibly imagine. You'd go crazy without it.

Yet because it's hard to do nothing at all, at least do things that are meditative in flavour. It's all about being in the present, and being sensual. Do things that involve sight, sound, smell, taste or touch rather than mental activity. When you become absorbed in gardening or cooking (assuming you like them!), you create your own harmonious micro-world with its own logic and natural rhythms. In those times, the past and future and the rest of the world gently fade into the distance.

A SUMMARY

If you find that spot meditations simply whet your appetite for a better quality of life, let me offer some suggestions.

- *The first is obvious: meditate longer and more frequently.*

- *Recognise exactly what stresses you and how much you respond to it. It's hard to continue self-destructive behaviour when you see it clearly.*

- *Examine your exercise routine, diet and sleep. If they're inadequate, you cannot be truly happy or healthy no matter how much you meditate.*

- *Remember that many things that give you pleasure also stimulate the body. Positive excitement has a very similar effect on the body to fear and anger. Try to be more moderate. Exercise some compromise in your ambitions. Go for a balanced life rather than excellence.*

- *Seek out those pleasures that also soothe you. Regard the simple pleasures of life as important. Make listening to music, cooking the occasional beautiful meal or wallowing in the bath part of your regular stress-management regimen.*

Oh yes, and be very inventive with your spot meditations!

INDEX

adrenalin 2, 6
affirmations 97–102
  Affirmation exercise 101–2
  for changing moods 98–9
  as chants 98
  for goal-setting 100–1
  to release tension while sitting 35
ageing 147–8
alpha brainwaves 71
anger 27
anxiety 4, 15, 17
  about the future/past 87
  and muscular tension 20
  and sitting 33, 48
  and the stress response 2
  and walking 51
  and yoga 65–6
attention, paying 104–8
  see also focusing
automatic pilot 104–8
awareness 29–30, 44
moment-to-moment 105–6

being 73
  see also present, living in
beta brainwaves 71
body
  getting in touch with for relaxation 2–7
  listening to the messages of 4–5
body scanning 36–40, 120–1
  Body Scan exercise 39–40
  effect of 37
  quick/slow 37–40
  seven stages of 37–40
  walking meditations 52
body-mind connection 2
books, on meditation 145–6
brain 70–1
Breathe Between Poses exercise 68
Breathe through the Stretch exercise 67
breathing 1–68
  anchoring the mind 25–6
  Breathing Freely exercise 26
  deep 15–19, 20–1, 25–6
    over-oxygenation from 18
    technique 17, 18–19
    while sitting 17–18
    while walking 18, 19, 50–1
  end of the breath 24–5
  focusing on when falling asleep 133
  free 18, 20–6
  for gym meditation 58–9
  hyperventilation 13, 14
  when ironing 113
  natural 17
  no-breath 14
  relaxed 7, 14
  sighing 8–11, 9, 14, 20–1, 24–6, 57
  for standing meditations 128–9
  synchronised 54
  tight/tense 8, 9, 13, 14, 15, 17, 54

for visual meditation 85
for walking meditation 47, 49–51, 54
yogic 65, 66–7, 68
Buddha xiv, 104, 105, 112, 117
Buddhism 65, 105, 145–6
Zen 75, 107–8

calm, false 48
centre of gravity 61–2
chants, affirmations as 98
chi kung 36
Christianity 98
chronic fatigue syndrome 15
classes, meditation 145
comfortableness 33–5
conversation 80–1
correct technique 138–43
Countdown exercise 40
counting the steps exercise 53

Deep Breathing while sitting exercise 18, 20–1
Deep Breathing while Walking exercise 18, 20–1
deep meditation 144, 145–6
depression 15, 48
desire 27
diaphragmatic massage 16
diet 146, 150
see also food
disappointment, regarding the results of meditation 141–42
dish washing meditation 113–14
distractions 30–1
coping with 41–5
identifying 42–4
Naming the Distraction technique 42–5
drinks 75–8
meditation 78

driving meditation 119–24
at red lights 119–20
Driving Meditation exercises 120, 124
noticing unsafe driving 122–3
in parked cars 120–2
safe meditation 123

Egypt 76
embodiment 75
emotions 27
endorphins 6
energy-fields 37
exercises
Affirmations 101–2
Body Scan 39–40
Breathe between Poses 68
Breathe through the Stretch 67
Breathing Freely 26
Countdown 40
Deep Breathing while Sitting 18, 20–1
Deep Breathing while Walking 18, 20–1
Driving Meditations 120, 124
Falling asleep 135
Food/drink Meditation 78
Going to the Toilet 117–18
Household Meditations 115–16
Naming the Distraction technique 42–5
Random Sounds 81
Red Light Meditation 120
Relax into the Pose 67
Sitting Comfortably 34–5
Snapshot 91–2
Standing Meditations 129
'Three Sighs' 20–1
Two-minute nap 134

Visual Object Meditation 86
Walking Meditation 96
Where am I At? 90
Where am I? 88

Falling Asleep exercise 135
fear 27
fight-or-flight response 2, 8, 13, 46
focusing 27–32, 38, 41–2
on active muscles in gym meditation 60–1
when falling asleep 132–4
on food 76
keeping track of 139–40
on little things 91–2
on living in the present 28–30
in open-eyed meditation 82–3
pleasurableness of 31–2
quality of focus 137
sensory in walking meditation 93–6
on sounds 79–81
in a typical meditation 30–1
on visual objects 84–6, 91, 94–5
in walking meditations 49–54, 93–6
in yoga 66–7
on your centre of gravity in gym meditation 61–2
food 75–8, 144, 148
Food/Drink exercise 78
overeating 76–7
preparation 109–10
freeze response 48
future 87

getting dressed meditation 112
goal-setting 100–1
Going to the Toilet exercise 117–18
gym meditation 55–64
attitude 56–7
coordinating breathing and strokes 58–9
focusing on active muscles 60–1
focusing on your centre of gravity 61–2
pausing between sets 63–4
the perfect stroke 59–60
stopping at exactly the right time 52–3, 62–3
Three Sighs for 57

happiness 99
health 99–100
hearing *see* listening
Hinduism 143
household meditation 109–16
Household Meditation exercise 115–16
hyperventilation 13, 14

imagery, for coping with distractions 43, 45
improving meditation techniques 139–40
insomnia 131–4
introspection, excessive 48
ironing meditation 113

Japanese tea ceremony 111

Kornfield, Jack 144
kung fu 61

listening 70, 79–81
focusing on sound when falling asleep 133
snapshots of sound 92, 94
to household sounds 109
and walking meditations 94

little things, sensuality of 91–2
longer meditations 144, 145–6, 150
love 99, 100

massage, diaphragmatic 16
maturity 147–8
meditation objects 29–30, 41–2
  urination as 117–18
  visual 84–6, 91, 94–5
  yogic 66
meetings, boring 126
mental busyness 20, 27–8, 29, 30–1, 41–5
mind
  anchoring in meditation 25–6
  focusing 27
  and insomnia 131–2
  projection of 80
mind-body connection 2
mindfulness 106
mindless states 140
mindstream (stream of consciousness) 29, 30–1, 41–5
moods
  changing with affirmations 98–9
  identification 89
muscles, tense 20, 65

Naming the Distraction exercise 42–5
Naming technique 106, 109, 115
New Age traditions 98
no-breath 14
non-doing/non-thinking 20, 73–4, 147

open-eyed meditation 82–6
  advantages 82–3
out-breaths, relaxed/tense 54
overeating 76–7

panic attacks 13
past 87
peace 99
Perth Meditation Centre xiii
physical exercise 146, 150
pleasure, nature of 111
positive thinking 100–1
powernapping 130–1, 134
present, living in 3, 28–30, 70, 72–3, 87–8, 104–8, 115, 149
  monitoring your ability 139, 140
  and walking meditations 95–6
present state, identification 89–90
progressive muscle relaxation 36
projection 80
public transport 126–7

quality of meditation 145–6
queuing 128

Random Sounds exercise 81
Red Light Meditation exercise 120
Relax into the Pose exercise 67
relaxation 3–4
  and affirmations 99, 101
  awareness of 5–7
  deep 3
  disappointment regarding 141–2
  whilst driving 122–3
  getting in touch with the body for 2–7
  of living in the present 3–4
  mental signs of 139
  monitoring 139, 140–1

physical signs of 141
practical 4
seeking out 144–9, 150
through scanning the body 36–7
through sensing 28
relaxation response 2–3, 130
retreats 109, 112, 143

scanning the body *see* body scanning
sedentary lifestyles 55
self-monitoring 140–1
senses 69–102, 147
comparison with thought 70–2, 73–4
focusing on 28
hearing 70, 79–81, 92, 94, 109, 133
household sensory experiences 109–10
and living in the present 72–3
relaxation through 28
sensuality of little things 91–2
smell 92
taste 75–8, 92
touch 70, 92
vision 48–9, 82–6, 91, 94–5
showers 111–12
sighing 8–11, 9, 14, 24, 25–6
Three sighs 20–1, 49–50, 57
silence 79
simple activities, making into meditations 106–8, 109–16, 117–18
sitting
comfortable 33–5
deep breathing for 17–18
disadvantages of sitting meditations 47–8
Sitting Comfortably exercise 34–5
sleeping
falling asleep 130–5
and focusing 132–4
insomnia 131–2
instead of meditating 145
to support you against stress 146, 150
two-minute nap 130–1, 134
smell, sense of 92
Snapshot exercise 91–2
sound *see* listening
spot-meditation, defining xiii–xvii
standing meditation 127–9
Standing Meditation exercise 129
stress
coping with extreme 142–8
knowing how to avoid your stressors 146–8, 150
positive 146–7, 150
stress response 2–3, 14, 46
and emotion 27–8
synchronised breathing 54

t'ai chi 36, 61
taste 75–8, 92
tea 110–11, 115
tension
affirmations to release 35
and breathing 8, 9, 13, 14, 15, 17, 54
as fight-or-flight response 2
muscular 20, 65
out-breath tension 54
scanning for 36
when seated 33–4
walking for 46–7, 51–2
tension-relaxation scale 4, 5, 7
checking 12
identifying your place on 89
mirrored in the breath 13

thought
  automatic 89–90
  comparison with sensing 70–2, 73–4
  contemplative 98–100
  identifying the content of your own 89–90
  positive 100–1
'Three Sighs' exercise 20–1
Tibet 110–11
tidying up 114
toilet behaviour 117–18
touch 70, 92
tranquility 22–5
Two-Minute Nap exercise 134

urination, as meditating object 117–18

Vipassana 44
vision 82–6
  meditations focusing on 91, 94–5
  softening 48–9
  Visual object meditation exercise 86

waiting 125–9
  boring meetings 126
  on public transport 126–7
  standing meditations for 127–9
walking
  comfortable 51–3
  deep breathing for 18, 19
walking meditations
  inward focused 46–54
    Breathing Deeply 50–1
    Comfortable Walking 51–3
    Counting the Steps 53
    Focusing 49–54
    Synchronised Breathing 54
    Three Sighs revisited 49–50
    traditional nature 47
  outward focused 93–6
    Being Present 95–6
    Sounds 94
    Visual Objects 94–5
    Walking Meditation exercise 96
    wind 95
weight-training 57–64
Where am I At? exercise 90
Where am I? exercise 88
wind, focusing on the 95

yoga/stretching 36, 65–8

Zen Buddhism 75, 107–8